A PARISH FAR FROM HOME

How Gaelic Football Brought the
Irish in Stockholm Together

A PARISH FAR FROM HOME

How Gaelic Football Brought the
Irish in Stockholm Together

PHILIP O'CONNOR ᔆ

Gill & Macmillan

Gill & Macmillan Ltd
Hume Avenue, Park West, Dublin 12
with associated companies throughout the world
www.gillmacmillan.ie

© Philip O'Connor 2011
978 07171 5018 2

Typography design by Make Communication
Print origination by TypeIT, Dublin
Printed by GraphyGems, Spain

This book is typeset in 13pt Minion on 16.5pt.

The paper used in this book comes from the wood pulp
of managed forests. For every tree felled, at least one
tree is planted, thereby renewing natural resources.

A CIP catalogue record for this book is available from
the British Library.

5 4 3 2

For my daughters, Ingrid and Freia —
it's all about the journey.

CONTENTS

FOREWORD

by Micheál Ó Muircheartaigh

They say one should never judge a book by its cover, but I am willing to admit that I was won over to this wonderful book by its striking cover. The location depicted seemed on the verge of a vast, uncharted territory, but the partial gap in the background trees invited curiosity beyond the unmarked, snow-covered football field. I became curious there and then about the content that would soon emerge from those pages which, strangely, may have started life as a sapling tree right there, in the heart of Sweden. Didn't we all learn about that trade while in primary school!

'Is ait an mac an saol,' I mused to myself, as I contemplated the improbability of a book extending well beyond two hundred pages that details the history of an infant GAA club 'far from home'. The team featured on the cover looked a seasoned one to me, and, at first sight, those stout-hearted Stockholm Gaels appeared to be in good humour. It was as if the playing season were just over, during which they had won many a hard-fought match. I noticed one in particular sporting a badge of honour on his ciotóg knee — the famous bandage proclaiming that the owner suffered from the dreaded affliction of a 'Croke Park' knee.

At any rate, I quickly ventured beyond the tree-line, and became fascinated with one of the latest of Michael Cusack's family members. Tá sé ráite riamh go mbíonn gach tosnú lag; Cusack's start in 1884 was indeed weak, and it took a while for the number of clubs in the new association of the GAA to multiply. There are now close to three thousand clubs, and the phenomenon is that over four hundred of those clubs are 'overseas'. They are spread around the world and they owe their origins to people like Philip O'Connor and his friends in Sweden. You see, Irish people of all generations loved their native pastimes and took them with them on their wanderings. The practice existed even before the founding of the GAA, and I discovered this fact while on a trip to Australia's Adelaide a few years ago. While there I was shown an advertisement in the *Adelaide Advertiser* of 1843, inserted at the request of Westmeath footballers, inviting a challenge from any other Irish county, or a combination of counties, to a game of Irish football on St Patrick's Day.

And now to Sweden's 'Parish Far From Home'.

I learn that they were once in a state of semi-panic when wondering how to make a team out of 'six or seven' players. But, with patience and the application of the Swedes' inherent love of orderly progress, one day or night the Stockholm Gaels club became a reality, and henceforth the Swedish-Irish and some of their friends from elsewhere had found a base.

It is easy for anyone ever associated with a new venture to visualise the problems that can materialise soon after the joys of the birth wear away. Where do we train while the snow is still on the ground? How about outdoor facilities when the days lengthen? How do we go about getting more players? How about opposition for a match, etc?

Those problems, too, were met head on; progress continued, and the great day arrived when a team from Gothenburg came to play a challenge game of football. The show was then truly on the road. Of course, it was a day never to be forgotten, as were the many other matches and events covered in this story which keeps unfolding.

It is all told in a convincing manner, with a clear message that the 'Parish' is much more than a vehicle for teams who wish to play. Parish members are now in fact woven into a community, and in this easy, 'read-along' narrative, one feels the presence of many wonderful people and characters who have become even better as a result of the existence of the Stockholm Gaels. It may indeed be a bit far away, but it has a communal link with some three thousand kindred clubs, radiating in all directions from Hayes's Hotel in Thurles, County Tipperary.

Comhgháirdeachas leis an údar, Philip O'Connor, *agus gach n-aon a chabhraigh leis chun an leabhar suimiúil seo a chur in ár measc*. Maybe someday we might see the 'Gaels' play in Croke Park.

June 2011

PREFACE

No one loves sport like the Irish. They say they do, but they don't. Having worked as a sports journalist and travelled a good bit and met people from all over the place, I can safely say that no other nation relishes or is obsessed with sport as the Irish are. Possibly the Australians at a stretch, but even then many of them have Irish connections to begin with.

It's not just single sports either. Irish people attracted to sport are interested in a breathtaking range of activities — everything from Gaelic football and rugby to tennis and Formula One. When the Winter Olympics come around, the pubs are full of pundits who have suddenly become experts in curling and bobsledding. Horse-racing is not only one of the most popular sports in Ireland, it is one of the largest industries in the country.

So it should come as no surprise that the Irish abroad have taken their love of sport with them. When forced into emigration by famine or unemployment, the Gael hit the trail with his boots in his bag. The Irish in America instantly took to games like basketball and ice hockey, and Australian Rules football bears such a resemblance to Gaelic football that both can be played side by side in the International Rules series.

But this story is not about sport alone. This is a story about what Irish emigrants abroad have achieved despite a lack of resources, despite still living in the shadow of our neighbour across the water, and despite being weighed down by the stupidity of some of the decisions made by our politicians. A small Irish community in Stockholm has come together, not just to form the Stockholm Gaels, but to use the network and goodwill that exists within it to help each other and other Irish businesses in these difficult times. And through businesses like that run by Lisa Bruton here in Stockholm, Irish manufacturers find new markets abroad.

In the globalised times we live in, emigration is no longer a death sentence. The combination of technology and cheaper international travel has made the life of the emigrant a lot easier than it was when the coffin ships left Ireland for America in the 1840s. Even today none of us takes the decision lightly to leave our family and friends and go and try our hand in another country. But if we do, there is no need to lose touch with them completely, and thanks to those who have gone before us, there is often a community ready and waiting to help us out on our arrival. Gaelic games are an essential part of that.

I invite you to read this story and take from it what you can: hopefully that will be something positive. Personally I hardly recognise the Ireland that has been portrayed in either the Irish or international media over the last year or so. I do not see the country or the people on its knees, completely without hope and its future mortgaged for generations. The Ireland I see is a young, vibrant and immensely talented country forced by circumstance to be better than the rest.

The future for Irish people at home and abroad is to rebuild the sense of community and caring for each other that made us great to begin with. In a recent conversation with Ireland's Ambassador to Sweden, Donal Hamill, we spoke about the ancient concept of 'meitheal' — if you help me with my harvest, I'll help you with yours. We both agreed that this is one of the key elements to both economic recovery at home and settling in a new country abroad. It is also the polar opposite of what got Ireland into this mess in the first place.

A final word to those now facing the emigrant trail, especially the generation which until now was spared the choice between the check-in desk and the dole queue. The Gaelic Athletic

Association (GAA) does not just exist in your home parish, where your mother and father, your brothers and sisters and your extended family are. There are GAA clubs all over the world ready, willing and able to help you and support you, should you feel the need to move there. Find out where they are and get involved on your arrival. Do not be worried about becoming enveloped in some sort of Irish cocoon abroad, because most of them will insist that you find your own way, learn the local language and customs so that you can truly feel part of where you are.

This way, you will find new friends and team mates who will do everything they can to support you. It won't exactly be the same as your home parish — nothing ever could be. But what you can do is band together with these people to build something new and vibrant that you can all be proud of — a parish far from home.

Be part of it.

Philip O'Connor
Stockholm
June 2011

| PROLOGUE

March 2008. The parade participants scramble up the ramp towards the door, a green-clad flurry of hats and scarves and buggies and children, all rushing to get off the frozen Stockholm street into the warmth of the pub. Inside the door pools of water have formed as hundreds of feet are stamped to shake off the snow, making the tiles as slippery as the street outside.

The mothers with babies take the seats around the walls as heavy down jackets are stacked up on window sills and stools, and a scrum of men in soccer and rugby shirts starts to form at the bar. St Patrick's Day is being celebrated by the Swedish-Irish community. Despite the number of Irish bars in the city, we are the guests of a Scottish landlord, who marvels at the mass of bodies from his vantage point behind the bar, safely shielded from the scrum. In spite of the biting cold outside, endless pints of stout, ale and lager are lined up along the bar. None lies idle for long.

Miriam is collecting the money for the Irish stew, and 50 kronor (about €5) gets you a spoon wrapped in a serviette which serves as your meal ticket. The younger lads are respectful but their only thoughts are for beer and craic. Most of them have only crawled out of bed in the past hour, so they either recently had breakfast or they weren't all that interested in eating after a feed of beer the night before.

With them stand some of the older hands, those who have lived in Sweden ten years or more. The children mill around, their cheeks still rosy from the cold under their painted-on tricolours. They add to the noise, dropping their spoons on the floor with a clatter and laughing as they chase one another in the tight spaces around the stools.

The stew finally appears, hot steaming bowls passed over the heads of the kids still running wild. It is wolfed down and the singing starts. With no instruments in sight, ballad after ballad gets an airing as songs and singers from all over Ireland have their moment in the spotlight. Poems are recited before Seán arrives. He sings 'The Fields of Athenry'. No one cares that it has been sung twice before. Some of the songs are the bawdy, raucous sing-a-long favourites; others are solos, the crowd joining in at the chorus. All receive rapturous applause.

Darkness falls. The mothers and children have long since gone home as Karl Stein calls for a taxi, and the driver is instructed to take us to O'Connell's pub in Stockholm's Old Town. We spill out of the car and pour into the pub where Karl is manager, and he starts pouring generous measures of whiskey for Irish and non-Irish guests alike. He turns up the music and we roar along to the Pogues and the Dubliners and U2 as the Swedes look on bemused. For them it's a regular Sunday night and they have work on Monday. For us there is no tomorrow; this is the high point of the year and one of the few occasions when the Irish community gets together to celebrate who we are. On this day we are inseparable as we laugh and sing and tell each other that we really should get together and do this more than just once or twice a year. For now there is a sense of belonging in the air, and for a few hours we hold on to it as tightly as we can.

A short distance away the body of a young man from Wicklow

lies in the cold, black waters off Stockholm's south island.
Another ten days will pass before it is recovered and he is flown
home to Ireland to be buried.

Chapter 1 ~

| GAME ON

It's amazing how easy it is to pick out Irish people abroad, especially on a sports field. Wherever we go, our jerseys are that bit more shiny and more colorful, our shorts that bit shorter and tighter than is decent, our legs that bit paler — a boy from Belturbet is seldom accused of being from Bondi Beach. Socks rolled down over our ankles, our football boots are only ever shiny when they are new out of the box; otherwise they bear traces of the muddy fields from whence we came. I'm hoping that the lads I'm about to meet follow this pattern as I head off out to our first training session at Gärdet in Stockholm, because for one thing it'll make them easier to spot. They don't disappoint.

I'm on time. Punctuality was never my strong suit before I left Ireland to move here in 1999, but all that had to change when I arrived in Sweden. When I was preparing to move, I was given one piece of advice from my good friend Earl McCarthy, who at one point held a multitude of Irish swimming records and was coached by a Swede, Glen Christiansen, when he went to the Atlanta Olympics in 1996. 'Glen told me to tell you something,' he said to me gravely in a Dublin pub before I left. 'He says that in Sweden they have a system, and you should always try to go with it. Because if you try to go against it, they will kill you like a dog in the street.'

It was not the kind of advice I was expecting when moving to a country famed for ABBA, blondes and Volvos. With the sharp warning ringing in my ears, my timekeeping has improved drastically since I moved to Sweden. But it obviously hadn't reached the ears of those I was about to meet. Naturally, they arrived 20 minutes late.

I'm sitting on a grassy verge when they come into view, all loosened ties and bags over their shoulders, hand passing a ball between them like overgrown schoolboys. They don't really converse like normal people; instead, all are talking at once, sentences running into each other, but occasionally all taking the same tangent at the same time.

'Is this it? This looks like it. Jesus, this ground is bumpy. You'd break your leg here. I broke my leg once, was out for months, never right again really. Look closely and you can see a lump. Can you see the lump? Have you got tape? I had some tape in my bag. Have you seen it? Not the lump, you eejit, the tape . . .' All the while I'm looking for the Kerry man, but as yet they seem to be oblivious to me.

Their sports bags hit the ground and they start fumbling in them as the only one standing approaches me. 'Phil? Nice to meet you. I'm Colin,' says the Kerry man at last. He strides forward and thrusts out his hand for me to shake, a glint in his eye and a smile on his face, as if this is what we've all been waiting for. And he was right. We had both been making efforts to get players together and maybe even form a team. And now here we were. It wasn't much, but as Joey the Lips said in *The Commitments*, 'It's a start, and I believe in starts, Brother Rabbitte.'

From the opposite direction a young, fit-looking lad arrives on his bike, all short haired and suntanned. It's no coincidence that he looks like an extra from *Home and Away*; he's an Aussie called Liam and he heard through someone at the local Aussie Rules club that a Gaelic football team was starting. He decided he'd give it a go and get in touch with the sporting end of his Irish–Australian heritage.

He picks up the round ball, looks at it quizzically as if wondering where the pointy bits have gone, and then smashes it straight up in the air before catching it again. He nods contentedly to himself as if he has unlocked the key to translating his Aussie Rules skills to the round-ball game.

Two more lads appear from the car park and I immediately take a shine to one of them as he is wearing a Dublin jersey; until this point I was in danger of drowning in a sea of culchies and Aussies, but here was a knight in shining armour, someone who would know what a two-lane road and traffic lights looked like. That he would later prove to be one of the best players I've ever played with didn't hurt either. John Carroll is his name and I'm delighted to see him, even though he has brought a Cork man to keep him company — which cancels out the benefit a little.

We make small talk as we get changed, and Colin passes me the ball as we warm up — the classic O'Neills All-Ireland ball, no different from the one we used in my last competitive game in some Mickey Mouse schools competition in Ringsend some 20 years ago. We're training on an American football pitch, so I saunter out the field a little and let the muscles dig deep into their memory.

With what feels like no conscious effort, I drop the ball and hit it sweetly. It flies over the bar in a beautiful arc, splitting the posts cleanly. I try to look like I meant it, but in fairness I'm astounded and the look on my face betrays me. Despite the lucky strike, I haven't fooled anyone into thinking I'm the ghost of Kevin Moran. It still feels great, but I can't help thinking it might be a while before I hit a ball as sweetly again.

Just how much of a task this will be soon becomes apparent. A few weeks before, I celebrated my 38th birthday, and despite not drinking or smoking and being in good physical shape, Colin and his lads are at least ten years younger. And with only eight of us taking part in this kick-about, there is nowhere to hide. The game of backs against forwards begins and I feel like my muscles are made of treacle as I try to chase them down. Time after time I think I have the younger lads in my grasp, only for them to vanish in a burst of acceleration and leave me grabbing at thin air.

We switch and it gets marginally better. I learned many years ago that in any ball sport the better the opposition the less time you have on the ball, so I resolve to pass it as quickly as I can and then move into space. But there's a problem: whenever I go to move into space, Mark O'Kane is already there ahead of me. He may not be the biggest man ever to come out of County Derry, but there are few quicker, and he nips in and steals the ball with annoying regularity. It's getting to the point where I would give him a sly dig if I could, but I can't get close enough to him to do even that. I console myself with the fact that it's unlikely I'll ever have to face him in a competitive game, but here on the grass at Gärdet it's cold comfort.

In the meantime Colin is flying around the pitch, a whirlwind of movement on and off the ball, dinking little passes with fist and boot, changing direction sharply, breaking to either side of the ball-carrier and screaming for it back. He reminds me of Michael Jordan, whose tongue used to stick out when he played. With Colin it's his jaw that swings open as he concentrates and calculates, finishing quickly off either foot when a chance presents itself. How he was ever allowed to leave Kerry is beyond me, but then the roads of the Kingdom seem to be littered with class footballers like him.

Thankfully, John Carroll is on my side. John is one of those ball players who always seems to have plenty of time when he gets on the ball. He's always in space, never apparently under pressure and always looking around for the right ball to play. It's like watching the Matrix when he gets on the ball, and time stands still around him.

He talks throughout, telling his team mates when to pass and turn and where to run, calling for the return pass and then sticking it over the bar with a minimum of fuss. If it wasn't for him I reckon we wouldn't have seen the ball all night. Eventually Colin calls time on the exercise and I collapse in a sweating heap, thankful to have had John on our side and that I will never have to face Mark or Colin in a game.

Despite the lack of fitness, we're all pretty pleased. Although it is apparent that we have some seriously talented footballers, the big problem is that we can't make a team out of just six or seven of them. The 2009 season is well under way for the GAA in Europe, but even at this late stage there is still an outside chance we can take part in a competition in Copenhagen if we can get enough players together. But that's a big 'if'.

We are in the chicken-and-egg situation that every new club finds itself sooner or later. To enter a tournament you need to have a sufficient number of players, but to get players to commit you need to have some competition to offer them. At the moment we have about half a dozen players and half a chance of a tournament, so we resolve to redouble our efforts, to put up more posters in the Irish pubs and contact every ex-patriot in our address books to make up the numbers. Even if the team we send to Copenhagen isn't going to win any prizes, it would still be a great weekend in one of the best cities in the world to drink beer — a decent enough prize in itself.

Despite the enormity of the task ahead of us, there is a positive spirit emanating from the group. There is good news from Colin that we can always go to the tournament and join up with other strays there. There are often B teams cobbled together at the last minute from the reserves to ensure that as many as possible get a game, so there's a pretty decent chance we'll be able to participate.

The lads chatter excitedly as we warm down and get changed, stuffing their kit into their bags and departing in the same direction from which they came, all suit jackets, shiny shorts and loafers.

———

Now that we're travelling, I decide to get serious about training. I'm reasonably fit, but after that session I am convinced that playing Gaelic football demands an awful lot more than 'reasonably' when it comes to fitness. There's a reason that Gaelic football games are 20 minutes shorter than soccer matches. The size of the pitch and the explosive, intense power and the use of the upper body required in Gaelic football make it much more physically demanding to play than most other sports. So I know I'm going to have to up the tempo if I'm not to make a show of myself in Copenhagen.

I'm looking forward to the chance to redeem myself on a Gaelic football pitch. Since being consumed by teenage laziness, the best years of my sporting life have more or less passed me by without my name ever being mentioned on the *Sunday Game*. But despite the fact that I'm approaching 40, I'm being presented with one last chance to prove to myself that I wasn't that bad after all.

I go back to lifting weights in the gym, something that hasn't ever proved too successful for me, but I'm going to give it another go nevertheless. A friend designed a punishing programme for me and my arms, shoulders, back and thighs all ache from the heavy sessions every second day. I seem to spend all my spare time eating and training, yet I don't see any results. Sure, I'm lifting more and running for longer, but other than that there are no outward signs that the training is working. It's not like I expected massive biceps and a six-pack, but I expected to see a little more of a difference. Still, as long as I can run and catch and kick, I don't need to worry about the *Baywatch* audition.

My stamina is increasing. I continue playing soccer three and four nights a week to get my fitness up, and where possible I play in the centre of midfield to make sure that I do the most running. The bike gets dusted down, the chain oiled and the punctures repaired, and as soon as the kids have gone to bed I hit the trail around the local nature reserve, going hammer and tongs around the eight kilometres to get back home as quick as I can. Even if I come up against an outstanding player like Mark O'Kane in Copenhagen, I'm determined I don't want to run out of steam. I don't mind a guy being a better footballer than me, but I can at least try to be as fit as possible and annoy the hell out of him. The only way to do that is to put the work in.

I worked hard all summer and I was hitting top form. I had honestly never felt fitter in my life. The training had helped my soccer game too. Not only do you get stronger from the training, but the increase in aerobic fitness means you get more oxygen going to the brain, which in turn means you make better decisions during the game. Simply put, because you don't get mentally and physically tired, you are less prone to making stupid choices as the game wears on.

But no amount of fitness and strength can protect you from everything, and it was during one of those soccer games that my 2009 season — and my chances of playing in Copenhagen — came to an end.

I turn out whenever I can for an English veteran pub team called the Tudor Arms, and on this particular Saturday afternoon I'm being shifted all over the park, playing at left back, centre back and left wing as we try to get a grip on our opponents, who are all from South America and handy on the ball. Eventually I get moved into central midfield and I start to enjoy myself. I don't see any more of the ball, but I do get to put in a few crunching tackles, something which doesn't go unnoticed by the opposition. And they would eventually exact their revenge.

Their goalkeeper punts a long ball down the middle, and being at least a head taller than any of their players I feel confident I'm going to win it. In my mind's eye I look like Paul McGrath as I leap up to head the ball out to our winger who is free on the right. I put the ball right into his path and I'm delighted with myself. But as I descend I feel the tiny push in the back from my opponent. The ball is gone and no one sees it, and it's only a little shove, but it's enough to put me off balance and pitch me forward as I land. The ground rushes up to meet me and I can't react quickly enough. My left arm gets caught underneath me as I fall to the ground, and as soon as I hear the 'click' I know it's broken. Immediately I know I won't be playing Gaelic football in Copenhagen or anywhere else any time soon.

A dull pain starts to pulse from just above the wrist, but I don't care about that. I'm furious and depressed in equal measure, but I'm determined to see out the last 20 minutes of this damn game, which we're going to lose anyway. Carrying my arm awkwardly I charge around the pitch, flying into tackles and sometimes even winning the ball. I run from box to box, desperately trying to get on the end of something and get a goal, knowing that if I do, it will be my last for quite some time. When our keeper roars at me to take a kick-out as he's done his groin, I roar back that I've broken my arm and he can take his own fucking kick-outs. I'm seething as he hits it short and our opponents pick it up in the middle of our half. I charge into a sliding tackle and win the ball. The ref blows up and I bellow at him, thinking he's given them a free. He hasn't. Game over.

I walk to the sideline and collect my bag, stopping only to stick my head in the door of the dressing room to tell the rest that I'm off to the hospital. Leaving my shin pads on, I change my shoes and walk over to the hospital across the street, still in my Tudor Arms kit. Thank God for the speed of the Swedish health service: half an hour later the x-ray confirms the break and the doctor tells me I'm out for a minimum of six weeks. The anger and disappointment bubble to the surface again. I call Colin on the way home and tell him what has happened and to take me off the list for Copenhagen. If the lads are going to start playing Gaelic football for Stockholm, they're going to be starting without me.

Chapter 2 ∽

THOUSANDS ARE SAILING

There is something uniquely satisfying about watching foreigners get their first glimpse of Gaelic games. To begin with there is the quizzical expression as they try to work out exactly what the hell it is they are watching: is it some bastardised version of 'proper' football, and if so why are they allowed to handle the ball? Is it rugby? Why then are they passing the ball forward and bouncing it as they run?

It's usually around this point that the quizzical look turns to one of horror, about the same time as the first tackle or shoulder charge occurs, and the stylish forward they have been admiring is sent sprawling painfully in the dirt by a brutish defender. All of a sudden this combination of skill, speed and savagery enters a new dimension of physical violence, and not everyone is comfortable with it. I have heard people groan audibly and watched them hide their faces as a hurl slashes into a thicket of legs in search of a sliotar, or a hulking defender pulverises a corner forward as he bears down on goal. Those of us who have seen it before are immune; it's going to take something special before we raise an eyebrow.

Such events usually mark the exact points where the individual quickly makes up his or her mind never to engage in either Gaelic football or hurling, and indeed to avoid the Irish as much as possible in future. After all, what can possibly be gained from hanging around with people who believe that such uninhibited violence is the best form of recreation?

Scandinavians in particular like to think of themselves as hard men — they are the original Vikings after all — but the macho self-confidence starts to ebb somewhat when the discussion turns to hurling. When they play ice hockey they do so protected by several kilos of padding on every conceivable part of the body, and a few of the inconceivable ones for good measure. Granted, the speed generated by skating adds an element of risk to hockey, but anyone seeking to diminish the toughness of hurling has never faced down a Kilkenny or Limerick man who has just had the sliotar nicked off his stick. With only a helmet, socks, shorts and a shirt for protection, simply walking on to the hurling field is an act of bravery that many hockey hard men would balk at.

But for those Scandinavians — especially those with a bit of a crazy streak like the Irish themselves — who decide to hang around just a little bit longer, they don't see them as dangerous activities. In this first glorious contact with Gaelic games they witness the opening of a Pandora's box of sporting possibility, finally freed from the constraints of other more conservative and less exciting games. Even if they don't understand it all initially, the chosen few buy into the idea that this is something they can do, an alternative to the staid and boring team sports that dominate the television.

Often for those non-Irish people who buy into the idea of Gaelic games, they can be hard to understand. For the Irish, they have been a part of us for thousands of years in one form or another. The sport of hurling, played with a stick and a small, hard ball, is woven into the history and legends of Ireland, and the stick itself was never far from the hands of the mythical heroes like Na Fianna and Setanta, the hound of Cullen. Sport and history are woven together in a way few other cultures can claim.

But the heroes of hurling are not limited to ancient history.

Legends like Christy Ring have ensured that hurling's mythical status survives today. In those regions where hurling is strongest there is almost contempt for the sport of Gaelic football: hurling is the sport of the artist, football the pastime of the artisan. To hurl well requires the mastery of hundreds of little skills and tremendous eye-hand co-ordination; hurlers see football as a brutish, less-refined cousin. Gaelic football, it is said, is a simple sport to play but a difficult one to play well. These are all obstacles to the outsider wishing to take up the games.

But it is precisely because of its apparent simplicity that Gaelic football is so popular in Ireland, and why it should be easy to export it far beyond Ireland itself. Its development mirrored in some ways that of the other mass ball game that eventually developed into soccer in Great Britain. But whereas soccer evolved as part of a long and complicated process, Gaelic football was first organised as something of a pressing cultural necessity. As the Gaelic Athletic Association (GAA) was founded in the late 1800s, its major concern was the preservation of Irish sports and cultural values. The Irish language and way of life had suffered greatly under British rule, but the GAA was about to change that. The visionaries who formed the organisation felt it was necessary to formalise the rules for football and hurling and to ensure that the games appealed to the spirit and the sporting nature of the Gael.

The differences between Gaelic football and soccer are fairly obvious, but some of the nuances sometimes get lost. Whereas soccer matches take place over 90 minutes and require great patience and individual skill, Gaelic football games are hell-for-leather, end-to-end affairs. That is not to say that Gaelic footballers lack individual skill; the basic skills of catching, kicking and tackling all require physical strength and co-ordination to execute them properly. Added to that, the massive size of the pitch exacts an enormous amount of stamina as well as a high level of intelligence to exploit the space properly. There is nowhere to hide on a Gaelic pitch: the ball can travel a hundred metres in the space of a couple of seconds, turning defence into attack and punishing any player not fully concentrating on the game.

The enduring success of Gaelic football and hurling is a testament to those visionaries who founded the GAA, and there are not many who can claim to have done more to cultivate Irish culture. Every summer people flock in their thousands to witness the tribal ritual of the All-Ireland competitions, where each county sends a team into battle in the hope of being crowned champions of the island on some glorious Sunday in September. These titanic match-ups draw some of the biggest crowds of the European sporting summer. Whilst our continental cousins close their factories and businesses and head for the beaches and their summer houses, the Irish make the pilgrimage to a football or hurling ground to cheer on the tribe, whatever the weather. Every parish boasts a local club, run almost entirely by volunteers, that is at the very heart of the community. Passions run high and rivalries are often as long as they are bitter. In many cases the slight that started the rivalry goes unremembered, but somewhere along the line it took on a life of its own and in the process became immortal. It doesn't matter what started it, why it started or why we want to beat them; what is important is that we beat them.

It should come as no surprise that a people that has travelled as far and wide as the Irish have taken their games with them. Forced to leave Ireland by famine and repression, first at the hands of the British, then the Catholic Church, the Irish are spread throughout the world. Still more fled the economic basket case that was Ireland in her first fledgling years as an independent state — a tragedy for those left behind but a boon to those communities they emigrated to. Sadly this will be repeated as the consequences of the recent economic crash make themselves felt. The economic migrants were and are often young and able-bodied and more than happy to play football or to hurl if it means a chance of a better job or digs in their new home town.

The thriving Irish communities in Birmingham and Boston, London and New York were fertile grounds for Gaelic games, and for good reason; thousands of emigrants were at their disposal, and in these new cities the clubs provided something of a social safety net to protect the Irish community. These clubs often had far greater resources than those back home. Being often the only Irish organisation in their area, there is no competition for sponsorship, and they can call on support from every Irish individual and business there. It's not unknown for players to be flown in and out to play key matches, such is the financial muscle exerted by these clubs.

What is surprising to many is that Gaelic games exist in seemingly bizarre places and sometimes with little or no Irish involvement whatsoever. The Norwegian town of Bergen has a Gaelic football team that flickers like a flame in the breeze, sometimes burning brightly, sometimes on the verge of extinction. At a recent tournament in Budapest, the Viking Gaels boasted a team made up solely of Scandinavian girls, many of whom had never been to Ireland. In the Brittany region of France there is an enormous interest in Celtic heritage and culture, and rumour has it that it is not unusual to find teams that don't have a single English-speaking player, let alone an Irish person, in their ranks. In Europe all of these clubs and teams fall under the remit of the European County Board, set up by the GAA to administer the games.

The GAA is one of the few examples of bureaucracy in Irish life that actually seems to work. Given the hundreds of years during which foreign rule was imposed on them, the Irish are not naturally inclined towards rules and regulations, and the fact that cronyism is rife in many aspects of Irish life and politics is a result of the 'divide and conquer' policies of the past. It is true that no organisation is perfect, but the GAA has survived and adapted to the changing political and economic landscape during Ireland's formative years and emerged as one of the dominant forces in Irish life, eclipsing even the might of the Catholic Church on its journey. The GAA is the original social network; long before Facebook and Twitter, the GAA was the glue that held people and communities together, a source of news and events and happenings that were at the very core of people's existence in Ireland, whether they be in a small town or a big city. Businessmen and politicians courted the favour of local club officials knowing that a good word from them could help them enormously. The local club was where you went to meet a girl, find a job or get an address for a contact abroad, should you find yourself on the emigrant trail. And of course as soon as you landed in your brave new world, you were co-opted into a new Irish community there, not so much removed from Ireland as transplanted to another small part of it somewhere else.

The major problem for many of us was that such a vibrant Irish community didn't really exist in Stockholm. Sure, there was a community that had lived here for a long time, and like everywhere else there were Irish bars that these people frequented. But given the nature of Sweden and its people, it wasn't exactly the most dynamic of ex-pat communities.

Swedish people in general tend to be very mannerly and somewhat conservative, and at times I think it would be difficult to find a people more different to the Irish. Whereas an Irish person sees nothing wrong with inviting themselves around for a cup of tea and staying for a few hours, everything in Sweden seems to be meticulously planned. If you want to visit a friend or neighbour, it's planned well in advance and everyone knows their role and what to expect; nothing is left to chance. The Swedes have great respect for people's personal integrity and don't go barging in on one another's homes. Generally they tend to be a lot more organised than the Irish. Then there is the weather. As a Swedish winter can last for up to six months, you're not likely to spontaneously stick on your woolly hat and just head off to the pub on the off-chance that someone you know will be knocking about. Socialising takes a degree of planning, which in turn snuffs out the sense of spontaneity for which the Irish are famous.

The only organisation with any visibility at all was the Swedish-Irish Society, which organised cultural events and an annual St Patrick's Day parade in the city. But a lot of the younger people, especially those with families, didn't feel particularly drawn to it. Many of the key figures had been living here for 20 years or more and society was taking its time adapting to the needs of the younger people moving here. There was no question that Irish people were looking for something to gather around, and Colin Courtney and I had no doubt that the answer would be a Gaelic football club.

———

For my own part, I grew up in an era where Dublin Gaelic football was the be-all and end-all of our existence. Some of my earliest memories are of being wrapped up in a scarf and brought to football grounds around the country as Heffo shaped his army into All-Ireland contenders. Sometimes we'd take the train but the more successful the Dubs got, the rowdier and scarier these journeys became and eventually we took to driving to the games in an old Ford Anglia.

Weekday evenings would be spent in Parnell Park near our home in Donnycarney on the northside of Dublin, watching club matches or the Dubs training. Our heroes were men like Tony

Hanahoe, Kevin Moran and Jimmy Keaveney, and I'd marvel at the enormous power the big full forward could muster as the shots he hit wide of the target thudded into the wall behind the goal in front of us.

My father was and is fanatical about sport, and he followed the Dubs obsessively during this period. At that time they were nobodies, but he was convinced that this team was capable of great things, something that kept him in a minority. Sure enough, that Dublin team went on to win two All-Ireland finals, and their titanic struggles with Kerry were some of the most exciting games ever played.

It may seem odd to some, but he seemed to lose interest after they won the All-Ireland he was convinced they were capable of. It seems that, for him, the joy was always in the journey and not necessarily the arrival at the destination. Nowadays he would barely look up at the TV if the Dublin footballers are on, but he will travel the length and breadth of the country to watch the Dublin hurlers. I hope to God he's right and that one day they'll be climbing the steps to lift the Liam MacCarthy cup.

Together with my grandfather and his brother-in-law, he instilled in his sons a love of Gaelic games that has never waned. Sundays spent in Dublin would often entail a visit to the park to kick a ball around, and the lane beside our house was the scene of All-Ireland finals every day when he came home from work. He was especially proud of my older brother, Alan, who at 15 was a bull of a teenager, tough as nails and strongly built with an aggressive streak and an eye for goal. Alan might never have become the player my father believed he could be, but he has taken those attributes and gone on to become a heavyweight administrator in the Dublin GAA.

As a player I fell between two stools as I languished in my brother's shadow both at home and in school. During my years in secondary school, Ardscoil Rís in Marino was blessed with some superbly gifted footballers, among them Pat Gilroy and Ger Regan who would both go on to play for Dublin. I played alongside them on the school team, but lacking a bit of encouragement from home I didn't have the discipline to stay focused in training and try to match their standards and workrate.

Whereas they would train every day with club or school, I concentrated only on the school teams due to laziness, often complaining that even that was too much. There are no short cuts in sport and even talented players need to work hard if they are to make something of their talent. Our PE teacher was a Galway man, Liam Moggan, and though he seemed more interested in middle and long-distance running, he was an excellent teacher of the basic skills of Gaelic games. He would line up the whole class, regardless of interest or ability, and patiently break down the basic skills of the game like kicking, punching and catching the ball. Even the better players benefited from his coaching as many of them had never been shown how to do these things properly before.

As a result of Liam's very fine coaching I became a competent player, but I was never going to be the kind of guy who would go and dominate a game the way a Gilroy or a Regan would. I was a bit of a show-boater, a great man to have around when things were going well but not the sort of fella who'd roll up his sleeves when the going got rough. At the first sign of trouble I'd disappear from the game.

A six footer at the age of 14, the teachers who coached the school teams deployed me at full forward or in midfield to make use of my height, and I always acquitted myself reasonably well, even if I never stood out. During PE classes we would play games of football and I would saunter around the field and then pick my moment to get on the ball, waltz through the defence and score a goal in a display of immense teenage arrogance. My team mates would expect the same when I played for the school team, only for my lack of fitness and commitment to be exposed when the stakes were raised.

The teachers eventually became frustrated with my lazy attitude and dropped me to the bench, preferring instead to concentrate on those more deserving for their efforts. In my immaturity I wanted to be one of the team's stars, but I wasn't prepared to put in the work and I gradually drifted more towards basketball where my height was to prove an even greater advantage.

Ironically, after I'd bitten the bullet and made the switch full time to basketball, my coach at the O'Connells Boys club, Finn Aherne, soon cut me down to size and cured me of my laziness, making me run suicide sprints until I was physically sick. He put up with no nonsense from me and even though our team was one of the youngest and smallest in Dublin at that time, we were certainly no pushovers. The senior players in the team were never indulged; instead they were given even greater responsibility for carrying the team forward.

With Finn there were no excuses. When you crossed the white line on to the court, the rules were the same for everyone. In truth, that season was a serious struggle, but it taught me the difference between not winning and being beaten. There were a lot of games we didn't win, but very few teams managed to give us a beating that year.

Hurling for the school was different. I had appalling technique, but I'd run like a madman and battle away as hard as I could, mostly afraid of getting hit if I stood still for too long. I loved the game, but it thrilled and frightened me in equal measure, and I never believed it was possible to take part in a game and emerge unscathed at the other end.

As a hurler the only real skill I had was being able to hit the ball off either side, and even that was wildly inconsistent. Once again frustration was to get the better of me and my schoolboy career would be short-lived because of it. Early in our under-16 season I jumped to catch a ball in training, certain that there was no one around, only to have my hand smashed by an opponent's hurl as I picked the ball out of the air. The knuckle on my right hand was split and bleeding profusely. The teacher coaching the team had no sympathy for me and let the play go on, saying it would teach me to protect my hand with my hurl the next time. I had other plans. I flung my hurl against the dressing room wall in anger and never played hurling for the school again.

I'd like to think they missed me on both the hurling and football teams, but that notion is laughable. I was one of perhaps 50 or 60 capable footballers and hurlers that were eligible to play that year, and no sooner had I gone off in a sulk than my place was taken by someone else. It's often easier to give up than to go through the growing pains and admit your mistakes, and in the end the only person who lost out due to my laziness and stubbornness was myself.

I continued to play basketball and soccer on and off until a persistent knee injury slowed me down. Music, alcohol and girls then came on the scene and I gradually lost interest in playing sport. Besides, I was sick of being told what to do and having my instincts curtailed by having to go and do the unglamorous work of defending or training. Like all teenagers, I felt the blame lay on everyone else, and that if I'd just been allowed to do my own thing I would have been a fantastic player and everything would have worked out fine.

———

When I eventually moved to Sweden, I saw it as a perfect opportunity to wipe the sporting slate clean and start all over again. For one thing, sport would be a good way to make friends and contacts in this new country; for another, I regretted all the years that had passed since I'd last played Gaelic football. I'd had a few seasons of soccer in the previous few years, but I was playing at a level far higher than I was capable of. At least by now I had a bit more maturity and could accept having to spend some time on the bench.

When I arrived in Stockholm in the summer of 1999 I wasted no time going to Irish bars to see if I could find a kick-about or maybe get a game going. But because most of the Irish lads worked in the pubs and didn't get to bed until the early hours of the morning, they weren't in any hurry to get up at the weekend to play football. Besides, by the time they did get out of bed, it was time for another shift in the pub.

There was the odd spontaneous game at Stockholm University, but it was hard for me to be spontaneous when I was living 40 kilometres from the city centre. It was also difficult to find a soccer team as the Swedes I knew had their teams settled and were reluctant to add any new players. As a rule, Swedes tend to make friends in high school or college in the area in which they grow up and possibly at their first job. After that they're pretty much done. They don't seem to have hundreds of acquaintances; a few rock-solid friendships seems to do the job for them.

I finally started a soccer team when I got a job at Reuters, the news and financial information company, and to this day I still give priority to lads new in the country when it comes to putting a team together.

Playing soccer was all very well, but Gaelic football was still gnawing at me. It was the game I really wanted to play. The further I travelled from home, the more important it was to me to do so. In 2004, five years after I landed in Sweden, I found out that Gothenburg GAA had set up a club. A quick search on the internet coughed up a mail address for them, and I wrote to Billy

Finn offering my services as an extra player for tournaments if needed.

A Limerick man, Billy is one of the many unsung heroes of the GAA. It is his effort and drive, and that of thousands like him, that gets clubs up and running and keeps them that way. He brings the same energy and commitment on to the pitch, and with him playing in defence and me in the forward line, we had many tough matches throughout our first season.

At the time I got in touch with him a few years ago, the thought of a Stockholm club was just a pipe-dream. I was prepared to travel 500 kilometres to Sweden's second city just for a game of football once or twice a year. He told me of his experience in setting up the club, the constant struggle to find players, get them out to training and games, and organising sponsorship and travel to tournaments. He didn't exactly do a great job of selling the whole idea, if the truth be told, but his knowledge was to prove invaluable when it came to setting up our own club in Stockholm.

Billy had been instrumental in setting up the Scandinavian championship, which was about to get its fourth and fifth teams in the shape of our side from Stockholm and our neighbours from Oslo. The plan for 2010 was to run it over four tournaments on four weekends during the summer. All the teams would play one another, with the two teams with the best record on the day meeting in the final. Points would be awarded to each team based on their tournament placings, and the team with the most points would be declared Scandinavian champions after the final round in Gothenburg at the end of August.

That was the dream, to lift the trophy in Gothenburg on a late summer evening, having played Gaelic football for a whole summer season. At this point in time is seemed a long way off, but at least we had a dream. And in sport, if you don't have a dream, you don't have anything.

Chapter 3 ～

| SOWING THE SEEDS

The phone rings in the cabin 500 kilometres north of Stockholm. I'm trying to work out how to get the frozen water pipes running again so that the kids can have a shower when they return from their skiing lesson. It might sound very posh, but skiing in Sweden is like riding a bike back home in Dublin, and most kids learn to do it at some stage. But instead of sorting out the frozen plumbing, I find myself on the receiving end of an ear bashing from a girl complaining about the lack of facilities for ladies' Gaelic football. In Stockholm, of all places. I'm starting to ask myself what I've signed up for.

The girl administering the onslaught is Anna Rönngård, recently arrived back in Sweden having spent several years living in China. Whilst there she had been introduced to ladies' Gaelic football and caught the bug, winning at the Asian games on a number of occasions with the Shanghai Sirens. She did not intend to retire just because she had moved back to Sweden either, and here she was demanding to know what my plan was for developing the ladies' game in Sweden's capital. Given that we hadn't answered her mails in good time, she assumed we didn't have one. I spluttered and thought to myself that if I could only focus her anger on the frozen pipes, we'd have our water back running in no time. I also decided that if and when we elected a committee for our new club, I wanted her on it. It was to prove a wise choice.

Ladies' football is a strange beast for us, given that most of us have little or no experience of it. It seems to be the polar opposite of men's football in our club. For one thing, the most loyal of the girls we manage to attract are in fact Swedish. Why they would get caught up in such a game is beyond me.

The myth that all Swedish girls are tall, blonde and blue-eyed is not something that holds up to scrutiny, and I have no doubt that girls here feel the same sense of uncertainty and insecurity about their appearance as anywhere else in the world. As I'm the father of two daughters, I'd happily support anything that emphasises the importance of attributes other than physical appearance, and ladies' Gaelic football seems to lend itself nicely to that. In Europe there is a very friendly atmosphere about the whole thing, competitive and supportive at the same time, and in the limited experience I've had, it doesn't appear to be at all bitchy.

Maybe the story of the players we were to pick up was similar to Anna's. When moving from Beijing to Shanghai she had asked the advice of some Irish people how to go about making new friends in the new city. Join the Gaelic football team, she was told, and sure enough she did, walking into a ready-made set of new companions just because she played football. Many of those who play with us in Stockholm seem to be searching for something: not just a physical challenge or a way to keep fit, but also a bit of team spirit and friendship and the kind of competition that, whilst serious, is not the be-all and end-all. Having trained in a downtown Stockholm gym for years, I'm well aware of the snobbery that exists as carefully coiffeured Barbies strut their stuff on the treadmills. In the initial discussions with Anna about setting up the ladies' team it becomes clear to me that to attract and keep players we will have to ensure a decent, friendly atmosphere where people can be themselves. That probably goes for the men too.

———

'How many d'you reckon there'll be?' asks Ronan, the owner of the Dubliner pub in Stockholm. He's writing 'reserved' on post-it notes and sticking them on the table in the snug of the pub we've booked for the first Stockholm Gaels AGM. It's a good question, but at the moment it's not one I have an answer to. I hope there are more than just the two of us.

After I'd broken my arm playing soccer, Colin and a few of the lads decided to press on regardless, and they travelled down to Copenhagen and amalgamated with a team from Belgium for the pan-European tournament. Having seen some of the other Scandinavian teams in action, they were all agreed that we should be able to hold our own and that the winter should be spent getting our act together and forming a proper club for the 2010 season. I was convinced that if this was going to have any hope of succeeding, it had to be done absolutely right from the very beginning, and doing things right in Sweden can be very difficult indeed.

Despite the massive bureaucracy — or, in some cases, because of it — Swedish society runs like clockwork for the most part. As the swimming coach mentioned, there are rules for everything: from what direction your car should be facing when you park it, to how you should queue for buying wine and beer. Going against the system is not to be recommended.

Whereas we probably would have got away with just mailing the GAA and showing up at tournaments, I wanted our club to be formed properly so that we would be eligible to book pitches, receive grants and generally run our affairs the way things should be run. In short, I wanted a proper club, even if it was to be located a long way from Croke Park.

In Ireland many of our clubs simply exist. They have been around so long that most of the members don't even know how or why or when they started. All they know is that the walls of the bar are lined with pictures of teams from back when men wore caps instead of helmets when hurling, and long shorts were all the rage. There is seldom a need to start a completely new club from scratch, and if it is necessary, say, in a new parish, there are hundreds of clubs whose experience can be drawn upon for help, as well as a wealth of expertise and support from people who have been involved in the GAA all their lives.

But in Sweden there are no experts and it would be the luckiest club in the world that had an experienced GAA administrator involved in the start-up. We needed to find out how to found a sports club, where and how to register it as a sporting organisation and what our legal and tax liabilities would be, among other things. Getting any one of these details wrong could see us being blacklisted by everyone from the authorities that rent out pitches to the dreaded Swedish taxman. And no matter how fluent you become in a foreign language and how much you think you understand the whole thing, the language used by bureaucrats is on a whole new level. And in Sweden they make no exceptions for anyone. This all had to be kept in mind just to start a sports club in Sweden. To affiliate ourselves to the GAA there would be a whole other set of forms to be filled in.

As the New Year was rung in and we started our fact-finding mission, I can't help but think how much easier these things have become in the internet age, especially given the country we live in. The Swedes are what marketing people like to call 'early adopters': if a new technology or gizmo makes its appearance, you can be sure the Swedes will be among the first to buy it, test it and probably discard it.

Broadband is everywhere, and the Swedes have taken to the internet society like ducks to water. It is virtually impossible for a business or a social service to survive and thrive if it doesn't make a serious effort with its online presence. The authorities have invested huge amounts of money in their websites and communications strategies: not only is all the information Colin and I need online; we can also fill in and send away most of the forms too, lessening the amount of time and effort it takes to get the job done.

Colin and I discover that to form a club there are a series of legal steps we need to follow. First we need to meet and have a founding meeting complete with an agenda and minutes that we both sign off on. This low-key historic sporting event took place over lunch in the Dubliner and lasted about ten minutes.

We unanimously elected ourselves as the interim board of the club until the first annual general meeting, which would be held in the snug of the Dubliner on 22 March at six o'clock in the evening. According to Swedish regulations, 'Every effort must be made to ensure that all interested parties can take part', so we put up posters in all the Irish pubs and spammed every Irish person we ever met with emails informing them. We weren't doing this just to satisfy the rules either; we would need every member, sponsor and volunteer we could get if we were going to make this work. The Swedish regulations are to ensure that everyone has a chance to have their say, but we have no interest in excluding anyone. In fact, given our experience of the previous year, we're more concerned that no one will show up at all.

You never really get used to the fact that, no matter what it says on the invitation, Irish people will without fail show up late, so my worries about a total no-show as the clock struck six proved to be unfounded. Anna was there ready and willing to take on the responsibility for the ladies, as was Colin, Ken Feely, Mark O'Kane and John Carroll, all of whom had attended the training session at Gärdet the summer before. Ronan the publican had stayed on to take part. No stranger to a sponsorship request, I'm sure he wanted to see with his own eyes what was about to happen. Seán Beatty, a true-blue Dub from Cabra, would leave his shift in the kitchen of the Dubliner to join us too.

Colin had also brought along a new arrival to Stockholm, Niall Scullion. Niall had arrived before Christmas on a secondment for Price Waterhouse Cooper. Given that he had recently played for the Antrim senior team and had done some of his coaching qualifications, he would be key to running a successful, modern club. He was a shoo-in to be appointed coach.

Jim Kelly and Karl Lambert, two faces I knew well from both the Irish bars and various official functions at Christmas and St Patrick's Day, were next to show up. Being from Longford and Wicklow respectively, it wasn't really surprising that I couldn't remember ever discussing Gaelic football with them before. I knew Karl was an avid rugby fan and a keen sportsman. Jim was a regular face at the cultural events organised by the Swedish-Irish Society. Like myself, Jim seemed to be here in Sweden for the long haul and I was delighted when he agreed to be nominated for the club's first committee. His command of the Swedish language and good standing in the Irish community made him a perfect candidate, and his sense of humour and organisational skills have made him indispensable.

There were a few faces I didn't know all that well, but there was no rush; I would get to know them all a whole lot better in the coming months. Karl seemed to be palling around at the meeting with a nice lad from Waterford called Keith. It turned out they had met in Swedish classes back in Dublin before they moved here.

Then there was James Guanci, an enormously strong young man working at the American Embassy for the US military. Despite his Italian-sounding surname, Boston native James had strong family ties to Ireland, reflected in the massive Celtic tattoo on his back that he had designed himself. James had never played Gaelic football before, but as soon as the possibility was suggested on St Patrick's Day he was on to it like a shot.

Noel Kenehan turned up to push the case for hurling and thus became a founder member, although he was soon to be transferred from Sweden by his job. His involvement was therefore short and sweet. He was told that we'd get to hurling as soon as we had enough players, but that for now Gaelic football was the order of the day. It's a simple fact that there are fewer hurlers than footballers. With the few resources we had, we would have to prioritise.

Colin and I passed around the typed agenda and followed the Swedish rules to the letter, informing the new members of our activities to date and electing a committee to replace our two-man interim affair. Colin and I were joined on the committee by Mark, Jim and Anna, and together with our members we laid out our road map for the year: to play a friendly against Gothenburg as our first game, then compete in the four rounds of the Scandinavian championship and maybe a round of the pan-European championship. All of a sudden we had gone from being a few lads kicking a ball around to a proper club. The first meeting of the club was brought to a close and all declared themselves satisfied with the proceedings as the future was toasted with pints of stout.

The rules required those elected to the committee to organise themselves. Colin Courtney proposed me as chairperson. Committee positions back home can be the subject of massive election campaigns as different factions in big parishes try to wrest control of their clubs from the grasp of their rivals. But there were only five of us in a club with about 25 members at that point. I was probably the most unwilling chairman in the history of the GAA. Whilst it was an honour to even be considered, it also meant a whole lot of work in the coming year. I had two small children and plans to start my own business, but I was going to have to bite the bullet. Together with Colin Courtney I had brought everyone here, and neither of us could back down now and expect someone else to take on the responsibility.

I had my revenge when Colin was elected treasurer on my proposal. Treasurer is a big responsibility, and treasurer in a foreign country even more so. Still, with his financial background he was happy to do it. Jim Kelly was elected vice-chairperson and Mark O'Kane public relations officer. Anna was given the position of club secretary, not because she was a girl but because she didn't really seem to be interested in any other position. Besides, the position of secretary carries a great deal of weight in GAA circles, and if Anna wanted to get the girls on the agenda and keep them there, she now had the right platform from which to do it.

As we sat around talking afterwards, I discovered that Keith Hearne, the nice lad from Waterford, had been living around the corner from me in a suburb of Stockholm for the last two years, and yet we had never met before now. I swore that by the time we finished we would put together a club and an Irish community that we could all be part of and be proud of. In that moment the single, recurring theme I would use for the year ahead became clear to me. I would repeat it in every speech and sign off every email with it. Simple, straightforward and to the point — 'Be part of it.'

The Stockholm Gaels were born.

———

The first training session had all the makings of a disaster. It wouldn't have been so bad if no one had showed up, but we sent out an invite and all of a sudden Gaelic footballers started to appear out of the woodwork. With the snow still on the ground, we booked an indoor hall in the suburb of Solna for the very first official training session of the newly formed Stockholm Gaels.

I collected the Beatty fella at the Dubliner and we headed off on the metro for Solna, only to discover that the hall wasn't where we (or I) thought it was. We got off a stop too early. A long march through the freezing snow and past some very threatening swans ensued as we sought to find Råckstahallen with only an iPhone and a dodgy map to help us. My patience was starting to run out, something that Seán took great delight in as he proceeded to wind me up even further. 'Are you sure you started a club at all? No doubt we'd be a great team if only we could find the bleedin' pitch . . .'

Eventually we made our way to the hall a couple of minutes before seven o'clock when we were due to start. By this time Seán and I were well warmed up. But the fun wasn't over. I could see through the windows as we arrived that everyone was still sitting in the reception. For some reason nobody had bothered to get changed and ready to play ball. Then it dawned on me. The hall was double-booked.

Anna and I went to argue with the guy at the counter, but it was obvious from his glazed expression that he wasn't going to do a whole lot to help us out. He ran his finger down the line of bookings a few times, as if ours would somehow appear out of nowhere, but no hidden secrets of the universe materialised. In the end he told us that they owned another hall in the area — quite close to where Seán and I had got off the metro, but still some distance away — that we could use, but he warned us that it was open to the public and that it might not be suitable. Given the choice between that and cancelling the training session, we decided to take him up on his less than generous offer.

We jumped into the available cars and headed to the other hall, pausing only to pick up a stray in a Gaelic tracksuit that we found along the road. Sure enough, the guy at the reception was right. It was indeed open to the public, but it was essentially set up for athletics and in no way suited to training for ball sports. But at this point I didn't care. I decided we were going ahead and quickly got changed, convinced that the sooner we got out there and started kicking a ball around, the sooner this fiasco would be forgotten.

We got changed and immediately started running passing drills to warm up, as kids circled us on the running track and skipped over low hurdles down the middle of the hall. The young sprinters soon found themselves having to avoid the errant O'Neills balls that thumped into the walls over their heads as we sought to reacquaint ourselves with the basic skills of Gaelic football. Not long afterwards, their worried coach displayed an admirable dose of sporting wisdom when he took them off into a safe corner to do some stretching instead, leaving us the run of the hall. He might have saved the career of a future Olympic medal-winner by doing so.

After some basic drills we split into two groups and started to play a quick hand passing game, using hurdles for goals. Though not exactly ideal circumstances, it was good enough to whet the appetite and the element of competition soon raised the temperature. Anna and Maja, a Swedish girl home on holiday who usually played in Poland, found that the previous gentlemanly conduct went out the window as soon as there were points to be scored, and they made sure not to dally on the ball as ferocious tackles flew in. With knees and elbows scraped and bleeding from the rubbery athletics surface, we eventually called it a day before a serious injury occurred. It wasn't perfect, but it was a start, and the things that we would need to improve on on and off the field were already becoming apparent. With the snow still on the ground outside and temperatures set to stay below zero for the coming weeks, the first thing we were going to need was better facilities — that, or a sudden thaw.

I'm not sure it could be called a defeat snatched from the jaws of victory, but at least we managed to get a training session under our belts. However, there was a cost: the double-booking put a dent in our credibility as we lost two promising Swedish players before a ball was kicked.

Over the years I had played a lot of soccer with Michael Halling and his brother Chris. Michael is a very skilful soccer player, a great dribbler who is strong on the ball, and himself and Chris go to the gym with the same regularity that Irish people go to the pub. Their grandfather on their father's side was an Irishman who was part of the great wave of emigration to America in the last century, so despite their having grown up in Sweden with little or no knowledge of Gaelic games, the two lads were perfect candidates. But when they arrived and found the hall double-booked, they soon got tired of waiting and headed off to the gym instead. We had lost two prospects who might have opened up a whole bunch of Swedes to the game. Michael did come to one training session later during the summer and though he was a very promising player, he never came back. A shame, because he definitely had the makings of an excellent Gaelic footballer, and might do yet. But if he is to do so, we need to sort out places to train that aren't double-booked when we show up.

The city of Stockholm boasts some fantastic facilities for sports from cross-country skiing to curling. Every winter an ice rink is set up in the middle of the city at Kungsträdgården and the general public can show up and skate around it for free. The city is dotted with *idrottsplatser*, sports grounds with everything from football pitches and running tracks to American football goals that can be booked by both clubs and private individuals. Indoor halls with climbing walls, goals and dressing rooms are also available; all you need to do is understand the complex system of who can book what and when to avail of them. Because we contacted the city towards the end of the indoor season, not only were most of the halls booked out; most of the outdoor pitches were also booked up for the coming outdoor season.

For a few weeks we lived a nomadic existence, practising the guerrilla sport of Gaelic football wherever we could find an hour free. As the thaw came and the weather improved we could use the bumpy grass pitches at Gärdet, but they weren't in the best condition and there were only American football goals. We needed to find somewhere to call our home ground.

We also needed to move on as a club in terms of competition. Training is all well and good but everyone wanted to see what we were capable of. At the AGM we had decided that one of the steps would be to invite Gothenburg GAA up to Stockholm to play a friendly, which would be the first game of Gaelic football ever held in Sweden's capital city.

Having been so helpful with his advice when it came to starting up the club, Billy and the lads were more than happy to make the five hour journey, and the date was fixed for the last Saturday in April. We had made plenty of progress in our first few months as a club and now we had a game to look forward to and a team that could compete. The immediate task now was to organise it properly and make the day something that everyone in the Stockholm Irish community would be proud of.

Jim Kelly and Karl Lambert had been volunteered by the rest of us to help with the practical arrangements, but we still needed to find somewhere to play. We wanted to make it a party day for the Irish in Stockholm, something we could all gather around that wasn't the St Patrick's Day parade, so it had to be held somewhere central that was easy to get to, and preferably not too far from the Irish pubs either. I threw the kids in the car one Sunday in March and drove around, starting with the various rugby pitches owned by the city.

There is a belief that rugby pitches are perfect for Gaelic football simply because the goals are the same shape, but that is often about the only positive point. To begin with, the crossbar is much higher than that of a Gaelic football goal. The pitches themselves are often torn up by marauding forwards scrummaging, rucking and mauling all over the field and consequently the surface often leaves a lot to be desired, especially early in the season. A quick walk across most of them was enough to rule them out.

I checked out the one Aussie Rules pitch I knew of, but apart from the bent and broken goalposts that were a danger to life and limb, there was a massive slope on one side of the pitch, probably not a factor when using an oval ball, but one which would cause the round ball to take on a life of its own. Another one written off.

But then I hit paydirt. I found a beautiful soccer pitch out near where I live — natural grass, dressing rooms, and plenty of space behind each goal where a ball could land without breaking a window or a windscreen. Even after the long, cold winter the grass seemed healthy. There was even a little wooden terrace on one side where the spectators could stand, and a kiosk where we could sell hotdogs. It was perfect, so the following day I made up my mind to book it.

In keeping with Sweden's wired-up, clued-in online society, the booking system for these sports facilities is internet based. Somewhere along the line a physical person will look after your booking, but first you have to find a time slot at the venue of your choice online. I sent away my request to the city to book the Akalla Bollplan for our historic first game of Gaelic football in Stockholm. The response came after about five minutes. Denied. No reason given; no suggestion of an alternative — just denied.

I emailed them back straight away asking why, and the reply wasn't long in coming. Grass pitches in Stockholm didn't open until after the May bank holiday weekend, and even so it was very unlikely that a minority sport like Gaelic football would have any chance whatsoever of being allowed to book them. Only soccer teams from the higher divisions were allowed to play on natural grass. Without having a national association backing us, we were unlikely to get preferential treatment.

Frustration with the Swedish system started to kick in as I envisaged having to go through the whole process again: selecting the venue, the date and the time I wanted, and sending off the request, only to have it denied for some obscure reason or another. As a rule it's the responsibility of each club to understand the booking rules and to be aware of the different periods when pitches and halls for the coming season can be booked. As a newly started club made up mostly of foreigners we had no idea and, besides, we were way too late.

But some kindly soul in the booking office took pity on us. Luckily for them they had the good sense to remain anonymous, for otherwise we would have co-opted them into the club and plagued them forever more. A booking was made at a place called Östermalms IP, a beautiful facility in the middle of one of the nicest and most exclusive districts of the city and a stone's throw from Stockholm Stadion, which was built for the 1912 Olympics.

Östermalms IP had a proper covered stand, a PA to make announcements, massive dressing rooms with hot showers, and a café. In terms of the goals, we would have to improvise, putting soccer goals under the American football posts to simulate Gaelic football goals. Soccer goals are a fair bit wider, but since I was going to be playing as a forward, it meant a bigger target to aim at; and given the way I shoot, that was no bad thing.

In the circumstances it was the perfect venue for such a prestigious occasion and it cost about €100 for the two hours we would need it. So we had a team, an opponent and a place to play. What we had to do now was make it a day to remember for all concerned.

Chapter 4 ～

| MARTIN AND ME

There is something very special about the moments that occur directly after a good idea pops into your head. I've worked with marketing and PR for years, and as anyone who has ever seen an ad on the telly will tell you, good ideas are like gold dust. When one does come along, you can enjoy it. For a few seconds you can sit there feeling proud and clever, knowing that the little nugget you are about to reveal will be a game-changer and have a lasting impact. I was packing up to go to training on a Wednesday evening in the spring when the idea came to me, and as I sent the press release out to the Irish and Swedish media about our first game, I knew I was on to a winner.

As the game with Gothenburg approached, I was investing more and more time and effort in the Stockholm Gaels: driving around looking at pitches, booking facilities and cajoling Swedes to try out the sport. It was becoming something of a full-time job. I had only become involved because of a simple desire to play the game, but now I was up to my neck in something much bigger than simply turning up and putting on my boots.

We had momentum now, and for me the key to using that momentum to build a club that would last could be summed up in one word — credibility. I wanted our first game and our first season to run like clockwork. I did not mind if we were beaten off the pitch in every game we played, because those things can eventually be put right by training and coaching. But if your club has a reputation of being simply a drinking gang or is otherwise disorganised, your endeavour is going to be short lived, especially in a country as organised and as concerned with outward appearances as Sweden.

A good example of how organised Sweden is when it comes to sport is that they even cater for disorganised drinking gangs that want to play football or hockey or any other sport. Called *Korpen* (which literally translates as 'The Body'), they organise leagues, referees, pitches and insurance so that all you and your pals have to do is turn up and play your game once a week — no further effort is required.

But we wanted to be a lot more serious than this. That was why it was important for us to get the club set up properly from the very beginning, to have proper accounts and training sessions and proper kit. For our first game we needed to cover all the bases and make sure everything went as smoothly as possible. Karl Lambert and Jim Kelly had been delegated responsibility for making it all happen, but everyone had their part to play.

We had a few sponsors on board, figuring that five sponsors paying around €500 each for the first year would be reasonable. We could have done with a lot more than that, but as this was our first year we didn't know exactly what it was we could offer them, so we decided to be a bit modest in our requests.

Given that there were two Irish bars, the Liffey and the Dubliner, looking to be involved, we needed to be sensitive to both. As a committee we decided we didn't want to exclude anyone, so we came up with a novel solution: when it came to social and fundraising events we would alternate between the two, but neither pub would have its name on our jersey.

There were two reasons for this. The first one is that the European GAA club being sponsored by a local Irish bar is almost too stereotypical for words. It seems that the first call every club makes after founding itself is to the local Irish bar to be measured for a set of jerseys. The Irish bars are tremendous supporters of Gaelic games and of Irish communities generally, but if we want to make a more wide-reaching impact we have to look beyond them. Not only should we be looking beyond the Irish bars, we should be looking to non-Irish sponsors in general who may have an interest in accessing Irish markets. It could be airlines or recruitment companies or estate agencies.

Secondly I feel that the bonds between sport — particularly the GAA — and alcohol are strong enough already and they don't need me adding to them. Sweden's alcohol culture differs greatly from ours, and I didn't want us to be branding ourselves as another ex-pat sports club more interested in beer and craic than winning games.

The sponsors weren't totally sure, but to be fair both bought into the idea. For our first game the Liffey would look after the hotdogs and catering for the game, with the Dubliner offering a meal to the players afterwards. Whatever this was going to cost would be offset by the amount of beer they would sell during the post-match party.

Even though we were working hard to get the sponsors on board, as a club we were still virtually penniless, but we would still need some sort of kit. Getting our own manufactured in time for our first game was out of the question, so I contacted my brother Alan back in Dublin to see if Ardscoil Rís, our old school where he was now a teacher, might be able to lend us a set of jerseys. They must have searched long and hard in the bowels of the dressing rooms there because eventually they sent over the same set of jerseys I had worn in my last competitive game for the school over 20 years previously. They were a lot tighter now with a few rips and tears from over-zealous students that had worn them since. Despite their historical value, the school didn't seem to be in any hurry to get them back either.

On the pitch things were looking very promising indeed: we had somewhere to play, we had a set of seriously retro jerseys to kit ourselves out in, and Niall Scullion, a former Antrim senior footballer, had a well-drilled squad at his disposal. It seems to be a feature of Gaelic football in Northern Ireland to play a possession game based on short passing, and Niall's philosophy was pretty similar. In his drills the ball was guarded carefully and passed quickly from man to man up the field to create scoring chances. He was worried about the challenge that would be posed by Gothenburg, a team who had been together for several years and had competed in Europe, but I had little doubt we could hold our own if we could hold on to the ball.

All that remained was to try to get the Irish community behind us and get a crowd out on the day to see what we hoped would be a remarkable spectacle. I enlisted Sandy, who looked after lunches in the Dubliner, to organise a tricolour to be carried on to the pitch by the children of the Swedish-Irish community. To make the atmosphere as authentic as possible, Jim and I would dig up the Irish national anthem from somewhere and play it before the game as the kids paraded the flag on to the pitch. Posters were designed and put up, and we created a programme for the day complete with a summary of the most important rules in Swedish for those watching for the first time. There was a palpable buzz in the Irish community, but it seemed that interest outside of that was quite limited. The wider world had taken no interest whatsoever in our sporting experiment. Here we were about to embark on our maiden season of a wonderful sport in a foreign country, filled with excitement and possibility, and yet no one in Sweden or Ireland seemed to care too much. That was when another idea came to me.

The trip to Paris brought out virtually all that was good in the bunch of Irish lads that travelled. Ireland had been drawn to play against France in a play-off to see who would make it to the World

Cup finals in South Africa the following summer. Ryanair tickets to Paris were bought for peanuts and tickets for the game acquired, so the trip was on. I drove down to the airport in Skavsta for the flight to Paris with Ronan from the Dubliner. In the departure lounge we met up with the rest of the travelling party: John Carroll, Karl Stein, who was managing the Liffey, Karl Lambert, who was sporting a ridiculous moustache which he was growing for charity, and about a half-dozen others. Many of them were soccer players like Paul Sullivan and Ciarán McCormack, who played for Långholmen, one of the main clubs for Irish and English ex-patriots in the city.

There won't be too many Irish sports fans who don't know what happened next. After probably one of the best Irish performances away from home, the game went to extra time. During this period the referee and his linesmen missed a blatant handball by French forward Thierry Henry, who pulled the ball back for William Gallas to score the winner and take France to the World Cup. That the referee Martin Hansson and his linesmen Stefan Wittberg and Fredrik Nilsson were all Swedes added insult to injury for those who had travelled down from Stockholm. From 200 yards away we saw Henry take the ball down with his hand and flick it back across the goal; neither Hansson, Wittberg nor Nilsson saw it, despite being a whole lot closer than we were. The final whistle went, and we were out.

A nervous French policeman I spoke to was bracing himself for the worst. He and his comrades expected the Irish to run amok having been robbed of a place in the finals by Henry, but once again the Irish fans conducted themselves with the kind of bawdy dignity that is all our own. Throughout the day the police had been puzzled by the behaviour of the Irish fans, whose only interest seemed to be in drinking, singing and taking the mickey out of everyone who passed them by. At one point riot police were deployed to clear a street in Montmartre to allow the buses through. As the Irish revellers were moved on by the police, one green-clad fan asked why the heavy-handed tactics. 'We need to clear the street,' said the gendarme. 'Well, you could have just asked us to move,' came the reply from the bemused Irish soccer fan.

There was no shame in our defeat that night. We played brilliantly on the field and conducted ourselves like diplomats off it — albeit very drunken ones. But Hansson and his linesmen were in the eye of a storm of criticism as calls mounted for the game to be replayed. By the time we got back to the Irish bar and saw the first replays of Henry's deception, Hansson was neck and neck with Cromwell for the most hated man in Ireland.

But a few months later I was about to give Martin a chance to make it up to us by inviting him to throw in the ball for our first-ever game of Gaelic football in Stockholm. The major problem would be how to get hold of him to invite him. With only ten days to go before the game, time was of the essence.

Aside from the publicity this invitation would generate, there was another reason behind the invitation. I wanted to get the attention of Swedes and everyone else and show them that the Stockholm Gaels was not just a club for Irish ex-pats clinging on to their culture. It was a club where everyone could play a part and feel welcome, regardless of who they were or where they came from — even the man who had cost us a place on one of the greatest sporting stages of them all. We wanted to stretch out a hand of friendship to Martin and his linesmen, who had been vilified and pilloried in the press at home and abroad, and to offer a chance to move on from his mistake in a sporting sense. Referees make mistakes, and so do players, but whatever happens in sport there is always another day, another game. Seeing as I was going to get the chance to redeem myself on the football pitch, why not him too?

Now the Irish probably don't need this explained to them, but as a football referee Martin is not the most popular man in the parish. Aside from missing Henry's handball, Hansson referees the Swedish league as well as top international and European club matches, so his name is often at the centre of controversies. It will come as no surprise that his number isn't in the phone book, nor is his address widely available. To invite him, we would have to go through the Swedish Referees Association. I sent a very pleasant and respectful email, outlining my reasons and inviting Martin to throw in the ball to start our first game. Realising what a stir this would cause, I sent out a press release to the Irish and Swedish media about ten minutes later informing them of the invitation, and headed off to training.

When I broke the news about the press release to the lads at training, the reaction was fantastic. I only wish I had taken a few pictures of their faces as they realised what was going on.

The credibility issue had many levels, and their problem in that area was the feedback they were getting from friends and family back home. Used to a much higher standard of play and organisation, many of them had got some stick from lads in their clubs for bothering with something as insignificant as Gaelic football abroad. People had no respect for the standard of continental club football, and figured it was something to do for an hour before going to the pub. Still more of them had got grief because their background was in rugby or soccer and they had only started to play the game since they left the country, or maybe they had no sporting background at all. It's one of the sorrier characteristics of some in Ireland that we sometimes feel the need to knock people, even for something as innocent as joining a football team.

But now all of a sudden the Stockholm Gaels would be on the sports pages and everyone back home would know who they were. We would go from being one of the smallest clubs in Europe to being the one that everyone was talking about, and if ever there was a doubt in anyone's mind about continuing and committing to Gaelic football for the season, this was the moment when it was blown away.

In the beginning interest in the story was cool enough. I had worked in communications and journalism long enough to know that thousands of stories hit the news desks every day, and the space afforded to the sports pages is always limited and hotly contested. But thanks to a friend, John Barrington, for a couple of days we would be one of the most talked about Gaelic football clubs in the country. John is a very good friend from Dublin who works as a sports photographer and journalist, and has an enviable network of contacts in the Irish sporting world. Though a soccer man and no great fan of the GAA, he still brought the story to the attention of several sports editors on our behalf, and it wasn't long before the story snowballed and the phone started ringing as the newsrooms in Dublin got on the case.

Over the following days I was interviewed by many of the national daily newspapers as the Gaels got a mention on many TV and radio shows, and the week culminated in an appearance on RTÉ Radio's flagship *Sunday Sport* show with Con Murphy and Jacqui Hurley. The mocking voices were silenced as support poured in for us from friends and relatives back home who had heard the story and loved it. We got hundreds of messages wishing us luck in the game against Gothenburg and for the future.

On the Swedish side there was a confused silence. I mailed some contacts in the Swedish media, but they seemed to treat the whole thing as a wind-up. I invited some journalists down to train with us and to get the whole story behind who we were and what we did, but to no effect. Despite Swedish involvement in the person of Hansson, it wasn't enough to generate much interest on their part for a minority sport. Meanwhile, Hansson and the referees association seemed to ignore the original invitation. Hansson himself was due to be in Stockholm on the day of the Gothenburg game to referee a match at the Råsunda stadium, so we figured it would be the easiest thing in the world for him to show up, throw in the ball and then head off to his game. I called the association again to see if he would be available.

Realising we were serious, the referees association scrambled into action and finally sent a response saying that Martin thanked us for the invitation but that he would not be able to make it. In his statement to us he called our invitation a 'great initiative' and wished us luck for the future, but as it turned out he would be on a train up to Stockholm at the time our game was due to start. Needless to say we were disappointed, but we weren't going to give up just yet.

Having seen the stir the invitation to Hansson had created, I felt I couldn't let the lads down and that I had to find a worthy celebrity replacement. However, given the short time available it wouldn't be easy. I thought of Johan Mjallby, the former Celtic player whom I had worked with on one or two events before, but he would be in Scotland at the time. I contacted Jesper Blomqvist, who had won the Champions League with Manchester United back in 1999, to see if he might be around. Jesper was working as a soccer coach for Hammarby in Stockholm at the time, but he was due to be on their training pitch when our game was due to start.

I was barking up the wrong tree. As I sought a replacement for Martin Hansson, I had become distracted from the original reason I wanted him to do it in the first place. Not only was Hansson a Swede in the sporting arena, the reason we had wanted him was because Irish people didn't like him very much after Paris. We still wanted to make a sporting gesture, to extend a hand of friendship, so if Martin couldn't make it, why not invite one of his linesmen instead? After all, they were at least as guilty — some would say more so — of missing the Henry handball, so one of them would serve the same purpose. Linesman Stefan Wittberg fitted the bill perfectly and, as it turned out, the Irish owed him something of an apology too.

Stefan may have been a contributing factor to what many will tell you was the greatest sporting injustice ever visited on the Irish people, but he was also at the centre of one of the more shameful sporting incidents to occur on our island. Whilst running the line during a World Cup qualifier between Northern Ireland and Poland at Windsor Park, Stefan was hit in the head by a coin thrown from the crowd and required treatment to a head wound. Given that the soccer sympathies of most GAA fans would lie with the Republic of Ireland team, there probably weren't too many of them in the crowd that day, but I doubt if that made much difference to Stefan.

Most Swedes don't see much difference between the Irish and the British, and the ordinary Svensson in the street has little understanding of the nuances of Irish politics. For them it's all just one big English-speaking melting pot. It doesn't help either that when they do show an interest in learning, we harangue them for not knowing the difference between a unionist and a republican. As far as Stefan was concerned, that incident happened on the island of Ireland, no doubt one of the more unpleasant experiences of his career. Not only would he have a chance to show his sporting side by coming and throwing in the ball to start the game; we as Irish people would have the opportunity to show that we were not all wild-eyed coin-throwing savages.

Inviting Stefan could serve another purpose for the Irish in Sweden. It could be the first step out of the shadow of our British neighbours and a chance to show ourselves in a whole new light. Despite the fact that their language is now our language, there are an awful lot of differences between us. If Ireland and the Irish are to successfully market themselves, then we need to make every effort to stick out and not to get lumped in with anyone else, be they British, American or Australian. Gaelic football is one of those things that makes us stand out.

Stefan must be slightly more popular in Sweden than Martin Hansson, as it was a good bit easier to find his number. My message was passed on to him by his son. When he finally managed to get hold of me he said he'd be delighted to come along. He lived close to Stockholm and would be officiating with Hansson that day. The media story was sent out again and it ran all through the week leading up to the game. Even if it didn't create as big a splash as having Hansson would have, there was still enormous interest in the game in Ireland.

The effect of the publicity back home was amazing. People in Ireland were calling and emailing their friends and relatives in Sweden to ask them if they had seen the story in the papers about the Stockholm Gaels, and as a result a lot more Irish people in Stockholm turned up to attend the first game.

I had been so caught up in the whole thing that I hadn't really had time to invite people other than a message to the members of the Swedish-Irish society. According to the Irish Embassy there are around 1,500 Irish people in total living in Sweden, but I'm not sure how accurate that figure is, given that there are no visa requirements and people can come and go as they please. What is true is that there is a large Irish presence in certain companies such as Ericsson, in addition to the usual Irish restaurant and pub owners and musicians that are to be found in most cities around the world.

What surprised me was the wide range of people that showed up: everything from English teachers to doctors, industrialists to bankers' wives. We had no idea that such a massive, silent Irish community existed in our city, and sure why would we? To date we had had very little to offer them, and until we did they were going to stay where they were, quietly integrating into their Swedish communities and getting their dose of Irish news and culture over the internet or in the pub.

The day of the first game was upon us, crisp and clear with the sun shining on the dirty banks of snow, the last remnants of winter ploughed and left to melt along the side of the pitch. I still hadn't had time to prepare myself at all for the game either physically or mentally. When Colin and I first met we just wanted to play, and I missed being able to switch off from all the media stories and the organisational responsibility and go and train and play football, but we were too far down the road now for that. I had made as many training sessions as I could and Colin and I had developed something of a decent partnership up front, but I wasn't really focused on the game. Billy and the Gothenburg lads had arrived the night before and everything was looking good, but even as the throw-in approached there were still lots of tiny details to be attended to.

Karl Stein, manager of the Liffey, was to be our MC but got caught at work, so Jim and I had to start the proceedings ourselves, running up to the little commentary box and connecting up a laptop with some music. Ronan had arrived from the Dubliner with a tank of helium and balloons for the kids, but after about two balloons the helium ran out and they all had to be physically blown up. Lisa Bruton had recently set up a company importing and selling Irish-designed products and handcrafts, and she had set up a stall for the day close to the pitch. Somehow she and her husband Per found themselves responsible for some of the hotdog duties as well.

Sandy arrived with a massive tricolour and gathered the children for the flag parade, and Max Tomsby, a soccer goalkeeper I've played with for many years, met Stefan Wittberg, our guest of honour, at the gate and brought him to meet the referee. We had two cameramen, Faisal Lugh and Robin Danehav, who would be filming the game, and Reuters photographer Bob Strong turned up to take pictures for us on his day off.

There were umpires to be nominated and white coats and flags to be distributed. Karl Lambert, by now nicknamed the Sundbyberg Express because of his pace and power, had been given the job of kitting out the umpires with green and white flags to signal scores to the referee, a task he took very seriously indeed. Together with a neighbour he went to the local hardware store in Sundbyberg and bought a brush handle and some green and white cloth and took it all home to his kitchen. Faced with the task of making four flags, Karl sized up the situation and in the absence of anything resembling a proper saw to cut the brush handle, he took the next best thing he could find and attacked it with a bread knife. Using all the knowledge gained from his engineering degree, several hours of hacking and sawing ensued before the fabric could be attached and he declared himself satisfied with the results as he handed them out to the umpires, hands still covered in red welts from the sawing. It's a shame the study of logic didn't form part of his degree; if it had, he would have walked the five minutes back to the hardware store and bought a cheap saw to do the job instead.

In the meantime, I ran into the dressing room to put on my kit and give a quick team talk after Niall and Colin had called out the starting 11 for the day. Such was the interest in the game, there were about two dozen players in our dressing room, as well as a few we had loaned to Gothenburg to use as subs. There weren't even enough shirts to go round and there were that many faces I didn't recognise that it was going to be difficult on the pitch. It was a great problem to have. Less than a year before, we were sending half a team in a car to Copenhagen to merge with Belgium. Now here we were providing players to two Swedish cities.

I told the lads how proud I was that we had come this far and what a great day it was for the people we were about to represent. I urged them to go out and to play fair. I didn't want to see anyone trying to cheat Gothenburg or the referee, and most of all I didn't want us to cheat ourselves. European rules allow for free substitutions, which means that players are allowed to enter and leave the field as much as they want, as long as there are only 11 of them on the field at any one time. In other words, there was no excuse for a player with tired legs to stay on the pitch. I told them that today could be one of the best days they had ever had in Sweden, if they'd only go out there and do their stuff.

There had been long discussions as to who should captain the team, and the unanimous decision between myself, Niall and Colin was that Kevin Carroll, a carpenter from Armagh, should have the honour. Kevin and his Swedish wife Hannah had spent many happy years together in Australia before arriving back to Europe. Hannah wasn't too keen on living in Ireland, so the family upped sticks again and moved to Sweden, something which was to prove a major shock to the boy from the County Armagh.

Kevin was having a hard time settling into the Swedish way of life until the Gaels arrived on the scene, but with the advent of Gaelic football in Stockholm, he could get out a couple of times a week with people of like mind, play the game he loved — and excelled at — and get it all off his chest. It made Monday to Friday on the building sites much easier to deal with, and it brought home to me that the Stockholm Gaels was about so much more than sport and a desire to win on the pitch. It was about sticking together and helping out one another off the pitch as well. I couldn't think of anyone that the captaincy would mean more to, and I was convinced that Kevin would be a brilliant example to the rest of us. He proved us all right on that front, and would go on doing so for the rest of the year.

A roll of black tape was produced and we made armbands

mourning the passing of Philly McGuinness. Philly had received a head injury in a collision in a Gaelic football game in Ireland the previous week. It felt like the right thing to do.

As we made our way out of the dressing rooms under the stand and out on to the field it became clear that this game had caught the imagination. The sidelines were jammed with members of the Swedish-Irish community. Panic. No CD with the national anthem. Jim and I had both thought the other would bring the music for 'Amhrán na BhFiann', but neither of us did and we were about to look very stupid indeed. Quick as a flash, YouTube came to the rescue. A search on the internet threw up a respectable version and we connected the laptop into the PA, so we were able to play the national anthem from the laptop as the children paraded the flag along the sideline where the teams were lined up.

The players broke away and took up their positions, shaking hands with their opponents as referee Liam Kennedy blew the whistle to start a minute's silence in memory of Philly. Liam had been involved in a hurling club set up in Stockholm some 15 years previously, which had abruptly closed down when one of the young men involved passed away. Here he was 15 years later marking the passing of another young man.

He blew up to signal the end of the minute's silence, then handed the ball to Stefan Wittberg. On Liam's signal, a shrill blast of his whistle which heralded a new beginning for Gaelic games in Stockholm, Stefan threw the ball high into the air between the midfielders.

Gaelic football had come to Stockholm.

Chapter 5

BORN TO RUN

W e wanted our club to do things perfectly and even if there were things we could have done better, in general the game against Gothenburg was a great success. However we would need to procure a set of kit pretty soon. Our visitors looked the part in their Azzurri outfits, whereas we looked like we were sponsored by a charity shop. For some of us, our white Ardscoil Rís jerseys looked like they were sprayed on to us. I had asked everyone to bring white socks and shorts so that at least we would be somewhat similar, but with all the colours of the rainbow on show we looked more like Oxfam United than Real Madrid.

At Niall Scullion's instigation, the midfielders and forwards had put their heads together and come up with a set play straight from the throw-in. The two half forwards and I were all to move towards the referee's side of the field, taking our defenders with us and clearing out the space in behind for Colin to run into. The idea was that we would win the throw-in and then play the ball quickly to Colin, who would use his speed to hopefully nick a goal. We lost the throw-in, and every subsequent throw-in where we tried to use that play for the next two months. Indeed on the one occasion when I started a game in midfield and won the throw-in, I didn't know what to do with the ball and promptly gave it away.

But when Colin Courtney knocked over the first-ever point for the Stockholm Gaels following a sweeping move that started with our own goalkeeper and built up from the back, we settled down and started to enjoy ourselves. Gothenburg were a little sluggish to begin with. The long drive and a few late-night pints on their arrival slowed them down as they tried to get into the game.

It was a tough game. Niall Scullion got a crack on the head, splitting his eyebrow open at the throw-in, and not long afterwards Carroll got decked himself. I walked over to help him up.

'Are you OK, Kev? There's plenty of lads on the bench if you're not . . .'

'Are you fuckin' kiddin' me!' came the reply. He had been looking forward to this game for a long time, and he wasn't going to miss a minute of it. He dusted himself down and played like a dervish until the final whistle.

Billy Finn, the driving force behind Gothenburg GAA, was marking me for the afternoon, and despite my serious height advantage he was tough, quick and difficult to make any progress against. As a result of all the fun and games it took to organise the day, I was lacking sharpness, waiting for the ball instead of going out and winning it. So I gave myself a bit of a talking to after Colin read me the riot act for wasting too much ball. I took my next chance when it came, beating Billy to a long ball over the top that landed between him and his goalkeeper and poking home the first goal for the Stockholm Gaels. It was an ugly effort, but it meant the world to me. For the next hour or so I could settle down and be a player like everyone else.

We continued to rack up the scores as Niall's quick-passing tactics paid off handsomely. We always seemed to have a man over in the attack to take an easy score, and the more we relaxed the more fluidly we played. But a wounded Gothenburg proved a dangerous beast, and they fought back strongly in the second half.

A wonderful solo goal from John Carroll put a bit of daylight between us again, and eventually the Gothenburg lads ran out of steam. We won handsomely in the end, but there were still things that would need to be worked on before we went to Copenhagen for the first round of the Scandinavian championship in a month's time.

But all that was in the future; we had a victory to celebrate. The players showered and changed and we headed off down to the Dubliner, where Ronan and the lads were putting on a meal for the players that had taken part. The regular Saturday afternoon crowd of late risers and soccer fans were treated to the sight of about 60 Irish people plus a few diverse other nationalities trooping in and spreading out, taking over most of the pub. The waitresses doled out plates of chicken curry as we tried to make sure our guests from Gothenburg were well looked after. As usual the children ran amok.

Brian Burns and his band took to the stage in the late afternoon to knock out a few numbers before heading off to do another gig in the city. Brian had lined out for Gothenburg during the game, where he successfully hid his sensitive artistic soul by going around administering some hard tackles in the half backs.

The music didn't finish with Brian's departure. A guitar, an accordion and a couple of tin whistles appeared and the sing-song started in earnest, with the instruments changing hands as quickly as the football had done earlier in the day. Niall Scullion laments the lack of a piano before playing a few songs on the guitar instead, and the Antrim man has a surprisingly sweet voice to go with the split eyebrow he sustained during the throw-in.

Max the Swedish goalkeeper throws in a bunch of protest songs from another era, and then from his seat by the window, the Sundbyberg Express started into his party piece, bawling out 'Seven Drunken Nights' at the top of his voice. I could swear some of the Swedes in the pub started to back away when they saw the rest of the crowd join in the chorus with wild abandon. Earlier in the day a bunch of individuals, some of whom had never met before, had gathered in the dressing room at Östermalms IP. Now, late on a spring evening in this Irish pub, they sat together as a team toasting their victory.

It was getting late, so I drove Maria home with our children. Such occasions aren't easy for her. We couldn't be more different, and where I have little problem with a roomful of people all wanting different things, she finds it difficult in that everyone knows who she is through me, but she didn't feel she knew anyone. Even Max, whom I'd known for years, was introducing himself to her for the first time. I was hoping the more there were of these occasions, the more comfortable she would start to feel.

I was happy to get out of the chaos for a few minutes. At home I picked up a crutch for Keith Creamer, one of the Gothenburg players who had taken a heavy knock to his ankle. As I arrived back in the door of the pub, he was standing on a table singing along with the rest of the lads, and the crutch would remain standing in the corner by the stage in the Dubliner for several weeks.

At about half ten the tiredness started to hit me. For weeks we had been working to get to this point, to pull together this whole fantastic project and make this day happen, and now I was exhausted. But what would be our only home game of the season had turned out to be a great success. The work wasn't finished. I would have to edit the video shot on the day in time for a screening at the Liffey a couple of weeks later, where all the scores would be cheered as if they were last-second winners in an All-Ireland final.

Billy and a couple of the other Gothenburg lads stood close by at a high table, and it occurred to me that from the outside the Stockholm Gaels looked like the happiest, friendliest, most successful club in the GAA. In reality, some of the lads who had played for us that day didn't know one another's names, and some of them we would never see again. But best of all was to see those that had lived in Sweden for 10, 15 or 20 years enjoying the craic and singing along, having watched a game of Gaelic football in the heart of their adopted city on a wonderful afternoon. We may have been here a long time, but for the first time it felt like the Irish truly belonged in Stockholm — and at last part of it belonged to us.

I always thought Roy Keane was a bit of a miserable bastard. I could never understand why probably the most decorated Irish footballer of all time couldn't enjoy his achievements a little more, and it saddened me to read in interviews that he enjoyed winning for a few moments only, but that he would quickly move on to the next challenge. I often got the impression that winning itself wasn't really what he was in it for; he enjoyed the battle even more than he enjoyed winning. In the aftermath of the Gothenburg game I started to feel the same way.

The day after the game there were another hundred small things to be taken care of: jerseys to be washed, balls to be counted and pumped, a barbeque to be returned. The party was over, and while the rest of the team were enjoying the hangover, I had taken Keano's lead and started looking to the next steps.

Our training for Gothenburg had been very thorough. Niall had come up with a perfect blend of fitness work and ball drills, which gave the players plenty of time to make friends with the ball as they got themselves into shape. But with only a month to the first round of the championship, there was still plenty of work to be done. We had played pretty well, but there was still room for improvement.

For my own part I needed more time to prepare, but my problems went deeper than that. Even if it was a friendly game, I was surprised by the pace and aggression shown from the very start, and it took me a little while to adjust to it. I'd scored two goals and two points and forced Billy to turn the ball into his own net, but the truth was I'd had a lot more chances to score that I hadn't converted. It was the same old story. Despite the passage of 20 years, I still had the same weaknesses I had when I played schools football in Dublin. I was a bottler, not prepared to put my head or my boot in where it would really hurt, not prepared to take the hit when it really mattered. Instead of trying to chase down a lost cause, I'd conserve my energy for later, hoping to be served up a chance on a plate that I could hammer home. Sure, I could jump for a ball and try to look like I was challenging, but the truth was I was beaten before I left the ground. And the worst thing was that any halfway decent player like John Carroll, Colin, Kevin or Niall would see through the points and goals I scored and say, 'Yeah, but when it mattered he backed down.'

They weren't the type of guys that would ever back down. Kevin might have suffered a serious bang on the head, but he would have to be run over by a bus before he'd leave the field. Maybe by taking responsibility for organising everything off the field I was trying to excuse myself for not taking responsibility on it. Either way I was going to have to be a lot more committed when we made the step-up to championship football if I wanted to have an impact and retain my place.

For the rest of the lads it had been a good exercise, not least in terms of team building. We'd beaten Gothenburg pretty soundly and played some excellent short-passing football, but there were some warning signs there. We lost our grip on the game either side of half-time, and if we didn't work hard and learn our lessons, our involvement at the business end of the Scandinavian championship could be very short lived indeed.

Unsurprisingly, we had cancelled training on the Sunday after the game, but that would be the last break that most would have until their summer holidays. In the meantime we set about making travel arrangements for Copenhagen, with the victory against Gothenburg putting the wind well and truly in our sails.

Chapter 6 ∾

DRESSED TO KILL

There are a few major differences in the way the Swedes and the Irish approach sport. For one thing, the Swedes seem to be happy to allow free substitutions, where players can enter and leave the field of play as they wish, allowing them to take a breather in the middle of a game. This is most likely a legacy of playing very intense sports like ice hockey, where players go in and play like madmen for a couple of minutes before going off and resting for a little while, and then starting again. Then there is also the aspect of getting value for money. If everyone has paid the same amount to play in a football tournament, then Swedish logic suggests that they get to play exactly the same amount of minutes, regardless of talent or ability. They are scrupulously fair in a way that we could seldom be bothered with. If you're good enough, you'll be on the field. If not, tough.

These two concepts are more or less alien to the Irish. With the exception of basketball, we grew up in a situation where if you got substituted, you were done and you took no further part in the game. For us, there was only one reason to be taken off, and that was that the coach thought that someone else could do your job better than you. There was seldom if ever a positive reason for being substituted, and the world is full of players who were right and coaches who were wrong when it came to making changes.

The Irish will also go out of their way to win any game or

tournament, and the idea that a guy should get to play just because he has thrown in his few quid doesn't wash with them. The best team should be out on the pitch at all times, and if someone drops below par they get banished to the bench. That's it, bad luck, but in the eyes of the Irish community, fair.

So there was no danger of any preferential treatment for those of us involved on the committee. With the first round of the championship approaching we were expected to train and work as hard as any other player in the team if we wanted to earn our place. But again, there were thousands of tiny details to be arranged, something that wasn't made easier by the fact that trying to get the Irish to do anything is like herding cats. Their strength of will and independence is such that you can't tell them to do anything, and most will see any arrangements you make as a suggestion that may or may not fit in around what they choose to do at any given time. There is also the possibility that they will change their minds at any given second, and a complete 180 degree turn would not be uncommon.

The first thing about our trip to Copenhagen would be to find out exactly who could travel. Regardless of the big turn-out for the game against Gothenburg, we weren't at all sure we would have enough players willing to give up a whole weekend and a few hundred euro to take part. Given that we were a fledgling club with seriously limited resources, there was a limit to the amount of financial support we could offer. For the most part players would have to pay for their travel and accommodation themselves. Like many clubs, ours covers the full spectrum, from businessmen to students, and whilst for some it's no problem to shoulder these expenses, for another person it might mean spending all their disposable income for that month on one weekend away at a tournament. For some it might even mean having to take time off work or missing a shift. Add to that the risk that playing time might be limited and you can see why some players weren't exactly falling over themselves to make up the numbers.

Thankfully, the result against Gothenburg had fostered a belief that we could make waves in the Scandinavian championship, and players quickly started to sign up. Under European rules the games are 11-a-side and a squad of 15 players can be registered for each tournament. As selectors and the committed souls trying to drive the club forward, Colin, Niall, Jim, Anna and I all signed up immediately, with Anna trying to pull together as many players as she could for a girls' exhibition game.

Our goalkeeper for the tournament would be Liam Ginnane. Liam is another of the love refugees who met a Swedish woman and somehow managed to let her fool him into moving here. As a chef who had previously worked in a Michelin-starred restaurant in Scotland, time off was hard to come by, but he did the unthinkable and told his employer he wouldn't be available that weekend — when asked, he couldn't remember the last time he had had a weekend off. His employer agreed, with the proviso that he was contactable by phone at all times during the weekend. It's probably fair to say he didn't take that condition of his time off all that seriously.

The single lads like Mark O'Kane, Karl Lambert and Ken Feely signed up immediately, as did Declan Graham, one of our pivotal players in midfield. Declan is a mountain of a man from Antrim and the first time I saw him coming to training, I dreaded the prospect of having to mark him. Even though he professes to prefer hurling to Gaelic football and has little interest in soccer, he is an extremely skilful player. He may not be the fastest on the pitch, but he possesses very quick feet and an even quicker footballing brain, a combination that enables him to escape from some very tight situations with the ball.

Nigel O'Reilly, a goldsmith from County Mayo, had also signed up, with his wife Tracey due to take part in the girls' game. Tracey had never played football before, whereas Nigel is an experienced and tenacious player with great speed and an eye for a killer pass. More than one opponent would make the mistake of thinking that Nigel's small stature made him a pushover, and every one of them would suffer the consequences of underestimating him. They had appeared a week prior to the Gothenburg game at the AGM of the Swedish-Irish Society, and were more than happy to find a fledgling club to play with.

The only Swede on the team was Viktor Widblom, an employee at the American Embassy who had somehow taken up the game and shown great promise in training. Three long-time Stockholm residents joined him: Barry Quinn from Carlow and Dubliners Niall Balfe and Liam Kennedy. Niall is an erudite and well-travelled man, and given his love of rugby I was surprised when he joined our club. But I can say I am enormously grateful that he did. His commitment in terms of both time and money is hugely appreciated, as is his razor-sharp wit and his immense dignity. Whatever needs to be done, Niall is among the first to volunteer — not to be seen to be doing something or to get credit, but because he thinks it is the right thing to do. He was one of the few who seemed to understand from the very beginning what it was we were trying to achieve, and he bought into it straight away.

Liam Kennedy was a bit more doubtful. He had been involved in setting up a hurling club some 15 years ago, only for the tragic death of one of the members to see it gradually fade away. A great lover of hurling and Gaelic games in general, he contacted Colin and me when we first got going and we all met for lunch in the Dubliner. As we ate, I got the feeling that Liam wasn't completely convinced we would or even could succeed, but the Kerry/Dublin double-act of Colin and myself got him sold on the idea and he threw in his lot with us. Not only did he join in the training, he also refereed the game against Gothenburg and planned to come with us to Copenhagen. He even offered to put up the money for a proper set of kit for us if he could have the name of his engineering company on the shirts. Despite being hugely grateful to Ardscoil Rís for the kit we used against Gothenburg, I wasn't too sure about turning up in Copenhagen in the 70s retro shirts with everyone wearing odd socks and shorts. But the question was could we get a kit quick enough. Liam outlined some of the difficulties he had when setting up the hurling club, and how hard it was to get things done. I gently pointed out that as a club we pay no attention to being told what we can't do. For the most part I'm only interested in what is possible, and at a stretch making things that *seem* impossible happen.

So once again off-field activities took over from on-field ones as we prepared for a tournament. And the clock was ticking.

I have been one of the first to lament how communication between people has moved from the phone to electronic written forms like email and text messages. The written word lends itself to misunderstandings, and what looks like a funny joke or an ironic comment in a mail can instead be interpreted as someone being an arrogant gobshite. Much of this can be avoided by simply picking up the phone and talking to the person instead. Having said that, I'm not sure Stephen Murphy at O'Neills was too pleased to hear from me when I rang him after sending a couple of mails in April.

Stephen and I had gone through the entire Irish schools system together, finishing up at Ardscoil Rís, and though we were polar opposites physically we were quite alike personality-wise. Stephen was a fantastic Gaelic footballer, a corner forward with such speed and technique that it was virtually impossible to get the ball off him by fair means and sometimes even by foul. He was also massively frustrating to play alongside, as he would always rather beat another man than play a simple pass for someone else to score. I always reckoned we could win a game by simply scoring the first point and then giving Steve the ball for the remainder of the game.

Both of us shared a love of sport and would talk the leg off a pot, which meant that the series of international phone calls we were about to embark on were going to be very expensive indeed.

When Steve left school he got a job in sales with O'Neills, the Irish company that is synonymous with Gaelic games equipment. When emails started to fly around about a school reunion, I noticed he still had an O'Neills mail address some 20 years later. Though he seemed delighted to hear from me initially, the old school Mafia was about to come back to haunt him.

I had checked around with various suppliers, including Adidas, a Swedish company called Salming and an English-owned company called Swagg in Stockholm to see if they could produce a kit for a reasonable price. Even though Liam had agreed to foot the bill, I wasn't going to go wasting his money. Swagg produced beautiful, high-quality jerseys but on closer inspection the Union Jack on the collar may not have been acceptable to all in the GAA, so I decided to skip them this time around.

Not that we had a whole lot of choice in the end when it came to suppliers. On closer inspection, we discovered there is a rule in the GAA stating: 'All jerseys, shorts, stockings, tracksuits and kitbags, worn and/or used for official matches, in pre-match or post-match television or video interviews and photographs, shall be of Irish manufacture.' This meant we were going to have to get a kit made in Ireland anyway. The GAA is nothing if not a political organisation and is very dependent on its rules and regulations, and the last thing I wanted was for the Stockholm Gaels to be stripped of a title or a trophy because we were wearing gear manufactured in the wrong country. There is a lot to be said for this rule, especially given the times Ireland is currently facing, but much and all as I support Irish businesses (seeing as I'm self-employed, I own one), if anyone ever tries to take a medal off me over the brand of my kitbag, they'll have a fight on their hands.

There are two aspects that make it difficult to do business with me. One is the fact that I have no patience whatsoever, and the second is I am utterly miserable with other people's money. That we didn't have very much of it made this part all the easier. As I dialled Steve's mobile number I tried to remember the last time I'd spoken to him, only to be interrupted as he answered. It felt like we'd only spoken the day before as we made small talk about wives and children and families and football before we got down to the nitty-gritty.

'Steve, I need a kit for the Stockholm Gaels pretty sharpish.'

'Grand, Phil, normal delivery time is four to six weeks from when you approve the original. We'll need payment up front, a VAT number, delivery charges, artwork and all the rest. The kits will cost about €50 each, give or take a few euro.'

'Super,' said I. 'But I need the kit by the end of next week. I only have a simple crest and I can't afford €50 per kit.'

A sigh from the other end of the phone. 'Let me see what I can do.'

I knew I was asking a lot and, to make matters worse for him, he didn't even deal with clubs normally. His job was to travel the highways and byways of Ireland looking after the big sports stores and making sure they were happy and well stocked for All-Irelands and Christmas, not dealing with bizarre requests from abroad.

But I didn't feel too sorry for him either. He was one of the few people in a position to help me, and I promised him that if the roles were reversed I'd do the same for him in a heartbeat. I also pointed to the great publicity we had got for our club and I promised that if he would help me out this time, I'd shout from the rooftops about how great O'Neills were. Their name and logo went on the Stockholm Gaels website immediately.

Ciarán O'Reilly had designed a crest for the club featuring St Erik, the saint most associated with the city of Stockholm, and we had given members a chance to have their say via the chat forum on the club website. Eventually we settled on a black and yellow design. We thought that the black Sligo inter-county kit was pretty cool-looking, so we decided that we wanted a black kit with yellow trim. Armed with this virtually useless information, the O'Neills design team went to work and created several shirt designs from scratch, complete with Liam Kennedy's logo and the website address on the reverse of the collar. It looked brilliant, and again the level of excitement and buzz around the club went up another notch. Now we had colours and a crest. We were another step closer to being a *real* club.

The Copenhagen tournament was due to take place on 22 May, but with a cloud of ash from an Icelandic volcano grounding aeroplanes all over Europe, it looked like our best efforts were still going to fall short. By 9 May — less than two weeks before the tournament — the design was ready to go and the order was dispatched to the O'Neills factory in Antrim. I don't know how Steve did it, and part of me suspects I don't want to know, but the Gaels kit somehow leap-frogged its way to the front of the production line and the match jerseys and a few replicas were produced in record time. The finished kit was still warm from the printing when it was packed into two big kitbags and shipped to the warehouse in Dublin. The race was on.

Another judgment call had to be made: where would we ship the kit to? If we asked for it to be shipped to Stockholm, there was a risk it wouldn't make it because of the ash cloud, in which case it would be better to send it directly to the GAA club in Copenhagen who were hosting the tournament. The problem here was that the expense of shipping the kit was starting to become more than the value of the kit itself. The only alternative was to find someone who would be travelling to Stockholm with

SAS who had a baggage allowance, or to pay for checked baggage for a Ryanair passenger. This represented our best chance of getting the kit in time and at a price we could afford — if the Icelandic volcano behaved itself.

Colin called O'Neills with his credit card details and they agreed to release the kit if we could get someone to pick it up. Colin had also come up with a 'mule' to check the kit in as their baggage to Stockholm. Dave Shanahan, a colleague of Colin's and the lads from First Derivatives, would be given the bags and he would then check them in for his flight to Stockholm. We've all stood through the series of seemingly ridiculous questions in Dublin Airport — 'Do you have any explosives in your bag, sir?' — but for the first time I realised the value of asking, 'Did you pack this bag yourself?'

Given the GAA's status as one of the most important organisations in the country, it wouldn't surprise me if O'Neills bags have the same status as diplomatic pouches and are allowed to pass in and out of countries unchecked. Dave dragged the bags all the way to Stockholm and the kit made it safely to Colin at his office. It was brought to the Dubliner and the two big bags were opened up so that we could see the shirts for the first time. They looked brilliant, and the members swarmed around like magpies hoping to get their hands on one of the beautiful black jerseys with the yellow trim, but we zipped the bag shut again almost as fast as we'd opened it.

Now we could go to Copenhagen looking like a proper team with a sense of pride in ourselves. And once again we were able to deliver something that most of the members thought was impossible. All of these little achievements were to become the building blocks for the bigger ones to come.

Chapter 7

FAR AWAY — SO CLOSE

I think Kevin Carroll might be dead. He crawled into the bunk above me at about midnight and hasn't stirred since: not a peep or a snore to signify he is still in the land of the living. I wouldn't normally share a room as I'm easily disturbed when I'm asleep; now I'm being disturbed by someone who is *not* making any noise. Under normal circumstances nothing will put you in my big black book quicker than a night spent listening to you snore. But Kevin appears to have gone into a state of suspended animation as soon as his head hit the pillow and it's a bit spooky.

I was the other extreme, nervous tension keeping me from badly needed rest. There are away games and then there are away games. Apart from the home friendly against Gothenburg, our season would be made up of drives of 500 kilometres or more to every tournament, with four or five games to be played at each. I was worn out from the drive down, but despite the tiredness I couldn't get to sleep, so I spent an hour or so checking mails and surfing before turning out the light at about one in the morning. Now here I was, awake again at six o'clock as the pale light from a dull May morning crept in through a chink in the curtains.

Dawn was breaking on a day for which we had waited a long time. The friendly against Gothenburg had been a great experience, but this was the real thing; for the rest of the summer there would be no more phoney wars. This tournament marked the start of something none of us ever thought we'd see — the Scandinavian Gaelic football championship.

The previous year we had the false start when we tried to get a team together and ended up sending a carload of players down instead because we couldn't make up the numbers. This time there were 15 well-drilled, well-trained players sound asleep in their beds in the hostel. When they awoke they'd be heading off to a tournament where they would receive their brand-new kit and go into battle for their club in its first-ever competition.

The drive down from Stockholm was a long one, but with the Swedes and the Irish mixing in the back of the minibus the craic was good. Those making the drive in Colin's car sneaked off earlier in the afternoon, and the real smart boys and girls were flying down, cutting the journey time from over seven hours to one. That left the rest of us to meet at about four o'clock at the Dubliner and load up the hired minibus with our bags, boots, cameras and our shiny new kit. Despite pleas for everyone to get something to eat and then go to the bathroom before departure, we were only an hour out of Stockholm when the first stop had to be made for a toilet break.

I had driven the road to Copenhagen many times before so I elected myself as driver, and up front to keep me company I had Liam Ginnane, our goalkeeper, and Gothenburg GAA's Eoin O'Broin. Tracey and Nigel from Mayo sat at the back with Niall Balfe, whilst the Swedish trio of Anna, Maria and Viktor occupied the middle row and spent the journey teaching the Irish contingent how to swear fluently in Swedish. The Danes and the Swedes have a healthy rivalry going on, and with the two languages being quite similar Maria and Viktor set about savaging the Danes and their perceived inability to pronounce their words properly.

Maria, whose job it is to teach Swedish to immigrants, has decided to help Tracey and Nigel with their language skills;

unfortunately for them she has decided to concentrate on the rudest swear words she can find, rather than teaching them something useful. Niall Balfe produces a folder with Niall Scullion's tactical master plan and proceeds to give it a bit of a hammering.

The booze ban comes under threat when Nigel and Tracey produce a naggin of whiskey and a drinking game begins in the back row, but there was no need to worry. To be forced to drink some of the whiskey the contestants had to answer a question wrong, and with three well-read gents like Nigel, Niall and Viktor, this was never going to happen. We couldn't hear very well in the front seats, but we did notice that Tracey started to giggle more as time went on. We assumed she was either cheating or in need of a book token as a Christmas present from her goldsmith husband. My money was on cheating.

The E4 motorway in Sweden stretches for almost the length of the country and we made good time towards our destination. We headed for the ferry terminal in Helsingborg for the short 25 minute crossing from Sweden to Denmark. Colin and his passengers drove on to Malmö and over the magnificent Öresund Bridge, but I figured that between the extra driving from Helsingborg to Malmö and the expense of the bridge toll, we were as well off to take the boat. We landed in Denmark and Helsingør just before midnight, and the town made famous by Shakespeare in *Hamlet* was eerily silent — until a minibus full of Gaelic footballers roared through it with 'The Boys are Back in Town' blaring out of the speakers and two Swedes roaring out the windows in cartoon Danish.

After another half an hour the much-maligned GPS signalled that our destination was coming up on the right, and a sharp turn through what appeared to be a gap in a hedge led us into the hostel car park. I've been to Denmark many times before and always marvelled at how they can be so different from the Swedes.

In Sweden society is very much based on consensus: everyone has to agree, otherwise very little happens, and every effort is made not to apportion personal blame. In Denmark it's a different story and a contrary opinion is worn like a badge of honour. If a Dane thinks you're an idiot, they will tell you, loudly and repeatedly, and nothing you say will convince them otherwise. They feel no need whatsoever to dress it up or make an effort to spare your feelings. You're an idiot, and that's that. Some people might see them as being rude, but given how hard it can be to get things done in Sweden, I find it refreshing but occasionally frustrating and insulting when I'm on the wrong end of it — like we were at the hostel.

We had made the decision to stay in hostels whenever we travelled to lessen the financial pressure on the club and the players, but hostels work a little differently to hotels. As we had made a group booking to secure the best possible deal, no one was allowed to check in until we were all present, and when we did check in they would only accept one single payment from the whole group. This was distinctly unpopular with those who had flown down and had to wait around in the lobby for several hours for the remainder of the group to show up. The rest of us thought it was poetic justice for the jet-set snobs, but this was hardly the time to tell them. Eventually Jim Kelly got tired of waiting and handed in his credit card, telling them to charge him for every room and promising photocopies of passports later. The suspicious receptionist behind the desk finally relented and allowed him to check in, a process he completed just as the rest of the group arrived.

Seeing the opportunities for a wind-up, the lads proceed to ask the receptionist the same questions over and over again until her cheeks flush red with barely repressed anger as she doles out bed linen and towels, whilst a laughing Colin goes through the rooming list and gives out the keys. The herding cats scenario begins again. People head off in all directions at once, often without saying anything to the rest, or indeed paying attention to what has been said previously. Despite the receptionist explaining to everyone about the extras such as hostel cards, door codes and linen, Colin has to answer the same questions time and time again, only for people to forget and come back to him to ask which room they are staying in and could they borrow a towel.

Despite the fatigue there's a relaxed atmosphere in the camp and there's not too much talk about tomorrow yet. Niall is repeating his mantra that championship football is a step up, and unless you're ready to go from the throw-in you can quickly find yourself lagging behind. The games are short and plentiful; each one lasts only 20 minutes, so falling behind in the early stages is not to be recommended. Other than that, he and Colin are giving nothing away. As the tournament approached I was involved less and less in the discussions about who should play and how we should approach the game. I was so busy renting minibuses and ordering kit that I didn't have the time or the inclination to be involved anyway. But as we headed off to bed I found myself in no man's land. I didn't know what was going to be expected of me, so I couldn't really begin to prepare myself for what was to come. I consoled myself with the fact that it would be a long day and I'd have plenty of time to fit into whatever the game plan was.

Even taking the drinking game on the minibus into account, whatever worries we had about our self-imposed booze ban were unfounded. Most were too tired to consider heading out on the town or having a beer in the reception of the hostel. Instead, they headed for the showers and bed as the clock ticked on towards midnight.

Kevin Carroll was still alive after all; I heard the tiniest whistle of breath from him. Even though I was relieved not to be sharing the room with a corpse from Armagh, there was no chance of going back to sleep now. I slid quietly out of the bottom bunk, careful not to wake the still-comatose team captain in the bunk above me, put on some shorts and a T-shirt and headed out into the overcast, chilly morning in search of breakfast. Thinking I'd be the only one up at this ungodly hour, I was surprised to meet both Niall and Liam in the corridor. The only two smokers in the group, they had to get up and head outside for the first fag of the day. We wandered off to the breakfast room, taking bets that big Declan would be the last to appear. He was.

The rest started to show up in dribs and drabs, with no one having any interest in being filmed by the video camera we constantly had with us. We created a cacophony of noise in a corner of the breakfast room as tourists from Scandinavia and Germany went quietly about starting their day. Karl, the Sundbyberg Express, arrived and attempted to quickly pass a motion that all snorers in future be forced to room together, given that he had spent the whole night awake listening to Barry raising the roof — good stuff out of him, given his penchant for sleepwalking naked. If anyone was nervous about taking part in our first tournament it didn't show.

Declan finally showed up for breakfast, which was the signal for the rest of us to get moving. We trooped back to our rooms and into the showers before getting changed. The brand-new O'Neills shirts would be given out when Niall and Colin announced the team when we got to the ground, so in the meantime we all threw on tracksuit bottoms, T-shirts and jackets and headed for the minibus, leaving a smell of tiger balm and liniment in our wake.

The address was fed into the GPS and we drove across a still-sleeping Copenhagen in search of the rugby pitch on Arsenalvejen that would be our battlefield for the day, and several u-turns later we find our way up the back street to the pitch. The local lads are setting up a makeshift bar outside the dressing rooms as others try to lower the crossbars to regulation height for Gaelic football. In the end the crossbars can't be moved, so two scaffolding poles are fixed under them and the nets hung. Part of me was getting edgy already, wanting to get stuck in straight away, just to have something to do. I'd been in Sweden so long that I automatically expect everything to start bang on time, and I was dreading having to wait around for the proceedings to get under way.

Kieran from the Copenhagen club welcomes us and shows us the schedule of matches that will be played on the bumpy pitch during the day. Our championship debut will come in the third game of the day against Malmö. Until then we'd have plenty of time to do nothing — not a situation that appealed to me.

There are as many different ways of approaching a tournament or a sporting event as there are athletes. When I thought I could make it at a decent level as a basketball player I got interested in sports psychology for a very specific reason. The free throw or foul shot in basketball is taken from exactly the same spot on the court every time. In game situations there is no goalkeeper, no defender, no wind, no external factor that can influence the flight of the ball or the outcome of the shot. There is just you, the ball and the basket, and whether you make it or not depends on what is within you. As a forward I found myself at the line regularly, so I practised free throws relentlessly. I was fascinated by the challenge of standing there with the ball in a game situation, blocking out everything going on around me and making the shot.

The bookshelves are filled with different theories from clinical psychologists and ex-pros to fairground chancers. They recommend different things ranging from positive thinking to hypnosis, and in the long periods of recuperation from a succession of knee injuries I started to read about them. Some authors suggested that it's best to visualise what you are going to do in a variety of different situations, so that you are prepared for them when they arise in a game situation. This was the point where my basketball game started to fall apart.

What happens if you start to visualise negative things? What happens if you close your eyes and you see yourself missing all those shots, or dropping your passes short? Surely that kind of visualisation is just as powerful as the positive kind? Some things shouldn't be analysed, and some weaknesses — like the odd missed free throw — just have to be accepted as part of the game. No player in any sport, not Michael Jordan, Tiger Woods, Leo Messi or Henry Shefflin, plays at the top of their game all the time because it's simply not possible. The key is to maintain a consistent level as close to that peak as possible. A Henry Shefflin operating at 90 per cent is still better than 99 per cent of the rest of the hurlers in the country.

A little knowledge is a dangerous thing, and I gradually started to erode my natural game by thinking about what I was doing far too much. The more I read about positive thinking, the more doubt started to creep into my mind, and I created problems where none existed before. Shots I would previously have made with my eyes closed started to bounce harmlessly off the rim. My ability to pass a ball through the smallest gap to an open man, which was my greatest source of pride, disappeared completely; every time I tried it, it looked like I was just giving the ball away. I went from being a free-scoring offensive player to simply being a tough defender, a shot-blocker who was hard to beat. For me, contributing at only one end of the court meant I was only half a basketball player. I was getting sick of sport. Not only was I going out on to the court or the football field and getting hammered by opponents, I was beating myself up for good measure when it was supposed to be about fun and competition and enjoying yourself.

The light at the end of the tunnel finally appeared when I heard Steve Collins talking about it on the television. Nicknamed the Celtic Warrior, Steve boxed professionally at super-middleweight, arguably the toughest weight division to make it in. He went to seek his fortune in America where he lost three title fights on points. Most people would have quit pro boxing, but not Steve. He returned to Europe and won the world title, successfully defending it seven times against the likes of Chris Eubank and Nigel Benn, boxers most commentators would have said were better than he was. In fact, following those three defeats on points in America, he never lost another fight.

During one period in his career he hired hypnotist and healer Dr Tony Quinn to help him in his corner, which had journalists worried that Quinn would have him so entranced that Collins could be beaten to death. He later talked down the incident in a television interview, where he said that positive thinking was a load of rubbish, and that the only person who ever won anything saying 'I am the greatest' was Muhammad Ali. 'A true champion does not believe he has a divine right to win every fight,' Collins told the interviewer. 'A true champion knows that every time he steps in the ring, defeat is a possibility. And he does everything in his power to ensure that it doesn't become a reality.' Finally, someone talking a bit of sense in a way I could understand, but it came too late to save me as a basketball player. Though we were both from the northside of Dublin, Collins was the exact opposite of me. He loved to train and sweat and work hard, to roll up his sleeves and get into the trenches and fight. When I met him years later in London, we had a long chat about Tony Quinn, hypnosis and the mental toughness required to be a boxer. 'The mental part is almost more important than the physical,' he told me. 'The physical is something you get over quickly. Besides, if you're a professional boxer and you keep getting hit, you're not going to last very long.'

From then on I combined the logic of Collins with the visualisation game. On the night before a match or training, I would see myself in certain situations and decide what I would do. Ironically, I stopped thinking about myself and my place in the game and tried simply to concentrate on doing the right thing in every situation in a game. Admittedly I still drift in and out of games, especially if I'm playing in a position that I haven't played before, and I will look at other players and think, 'Shit, I hope he doesn't end up marking me.' When he does, I use another Collins trick. 'Find a weakness,' he says. 'Everyone has one somewhere, and when you find it, hammer it.' For the next hour or so I would have to look at the other four teams and find the weaknesses. It wouldn't be easy.

'Lads, with five teams playing it means we'll get a chance to see the other four in action before getting in the ring. That's good. This way we'll know what to expect,' says Niall as he gathers everyone around. I'm watching the tough-looking lads taking the field for the opening game and the Celtic Warrior pops into my head. I decide I'm not going to stand here admiring these other fellas; instead I'm going to watch them closely. I'm going to find a weakness and then I'm going to hammer it.

We gather at the back of the minibus as Niall starts to distribute the shirts and tells us our starting positions for the day. We stand around fidgeting like small boys, hoping our names will be called out among the first 11 and preparing to hide our disappointment if they are not. My name is the last of the 11 to be called out. I'll be playing up front alongside Colin.

For now, Gothenburg are our barometer, the only other team we have seen play and we eagerly await the throw-in in the first game between Malmö and Copenhagen. Malmö burst on to the scene the previous year and won the championship at the first attempt, whereas Copenhagen were the holders of the European Shield. Even if it is the second-tier competition in European terms, it's still a marvellous achievement and a warning to other teams not to take them lightly.

The game proves to be a tough, physical encounter. Apparently

The author and ladies' captain, Anna Rönngård. A former Asian champion with the Shanghai Sirens, Swede Anna is the driving force behind ladies' football in the club.

The author and Swedish soccer official Stefan Wittberg, who atoned for the miss that cost Ireland a place in the soccer World Cup by throwing in the ball for our first game in April 2010.

The children of the Swedish-Irish community parade the tricolour before our first game. (*Courtesy of Bob Strong*)

Niall Scullion sizes up his options as Eoin O'Broin (17) and former Cork City soccer player Mark O'Sullivan (16) move in. (*Courtesy of Bob Strong*)

Big Declan Graham steals the ball in mid-air from Gothenburg's Keith Creamer. (*Courtesy of Bob Strong*)

Gothenburg's free-scoring Adrian Kelly takes on Don Corry in our first game. (*Courtesy of Bob Strong*)

Former Antrim inter-county player Niall Scullion tries to avoid the clutches of his namesake, Niall O'Connor. (*Courtesy of Bob Strong*)

John Carroll leaves the opposition clutching at thin air. (*Courtesy of Bob Strong*)

Declan Graham juggles the ball as the Gaels relax before meeting Gothenburg. (*Courtesy of Tracey Sweeney*)

The Copenhagen GAA team photo taken at their home tournament, May 2010. (*Courtesy of Liam Kennedy*)

The Malmö team photo from the opening tournament in Copenhagen, with Brian Boyd's pink shorts on view (*back row, second right*). (*Courtesy of Liam Kennedy*)

Gothenburg's team photo from the Copenhagen tournament, with Billy Finn at the centre of the front row. (*Courtesy of Liam Kennedy*)

Malmö's Martin Long wins the throw-in against Declan Graham in our first game in Copenhagen. (*Courtesy of Liam Kennedy*)

The Oslo team huddle at their first tournament in Copenhagen. (*Courtesy of Tracey Sweeney*)

Sponsor, referee and emergency centre forward Liam Kennedy enjoys a joke with Ken Feely and the author (11), as Colin Courtney (10) watches the action unfold in Copenhagen. (*Courtesy of Tracey Sweeney*)

Deceptively quick for a big man, Declan Graham makes space against Oslo in a must-win game in Copenhagen. (*Courtesy of Tracey Sweeney*)

Ken Feely (*right*) talks to Viktor Widblom, the sole Swede to represent the Gaels during the season.

The 'Sundbyberg Express' (3) and Mark O'Kane have a much-needed drink as the temperature rises in Copenhagen. (*Courtesy of Tracey Sweeney*)

Gaels in the Hood (*left to right*): Karl Lambert, Declan Graham, Nigel O'Reilly, Niall Scullion and Liam Ginnane seek shade from the sun in Denmark. (*Courtesy of Tracey Sweeney*)

Aidan 'Ginge' O'Reilly (black tracksuit top) leads the Malmö warm-up at their home tournament. (*Courtesy of Colin Cotter*)

Oslo GAA's Freddie (*right*) towers over all as referee Shay O'Doherty tosses the coin. (*Courtesy of Colin Cotter*)

James Guanci (*right*) lines out with his temporary team mates from Gothenburg, where he was loaned out to gain valuable match experience. (*Courtesy of Colin Cotter*)

Big James Guanci (white shorts) saw plenty of action as he was loaned out to Gothenburg at the Malmö tournament. He returned to Stockholm later in the day and played a key role in the defeat of Copenhagen. (*Courtesy of Colin Cotter*)

Gothenburg's massed ranks admiring an Oslo clearance. (*Courtesy of Colin Cotter*)

The Stockholm Gaels team that won the Malmö tournament, beating the hosts in the final. *Back row, left to right*: Keith Hearne, Ken Feely, Karl 'Sundbyberg Express' Lambert, the author, Liam Ginnane, Seán Beatty, Declan Graham, Jim Kelly. *Front row*: John Carroll, Kevin Carroll, Mark O'Kane, Colin Courtney, Niall Scullion, Niall Balfe, Ciarán O'Reilly. (*Courtesy of Colin Cotter*)

A truly international sports day in Malmö. On one side of our Gaelic football tournament was Aussie Rules, on the other a cricket match in the shadow of the 'Turning Tower'. (*Courtesy of Colin Cotter*)

Declan Graham (6) and Brian Boyd (8)—now with his normal-coloured shorts—contest the throw-in in Malmö. (*Courtesy of Colin Cotter*)

The injured Barry Quinn documents the efforts of his team mates using a video camera. (*Courtesy of Colin Cotter*)

there is a bit of history between the two teams going back over previous tournaments, and no quarter is asked or given on either side. The referee for the day is John Kelleher, who has been involved in Copenhagen GAA from the very beginning. John is not in a hurry to blow his whistle and seems content to let the rough stuff go if a team retains possession — and sometimes even if they don't. I decide I'm not going to go looking for any protection from him. Though my inner coward is alive and well, I'm going to go in and take whatever rough stuff these guys are going to dish out. Time to stand up and be counted.

The game remains close fought all the way through, and in something of a surprise given that Copenhagen were at home, Malmö eventually run out winners by the slimmest of margins, 0-5 to 0-4, to set themselves up nicely for the day. Copenhagen will have to fight hard to get themselves back in the running after this setback against probably their biggest rivals. It will be all uphill from here.

Next up is Gothenburg versus the other club making its debut, Oslo. The Norwegians have had a long journey down and arrived both hung over and a bit short handed, so they borrow a couple of lads from Copenhagen to make up their team. They also boast probably the biggest human being I have ever seen in their midfield, a young Norwegian called Freddie, a massive, blond, youthful hulk who was discovered celebrating St Patrick's Day in an Irish pub in Oslo and is fast becoming a GAA legend. The story goes that when the lads at Oslo GAA met him in the pub and saw the size of his hands, they decided they had to have him in the team. Not only is Freddie absolutely huge, he is also stone mad, and being up for just about anything, he duly obliged by joining them. Big and strong with a firm grasp of the fundamentals of the game, Freddie masks his lack of speed and finesse by bulldozing his way around the field to good effect, even if his reckless streak is worrying.

The old hands of Gothenburg have too much experience for the new club and they quickly get a grip on the game. In fine form in the forward line, they start to build up a lead as the Norwegians suffer in front of goal. In their eagerness to establish themselves, they make a few bad decisions and waste some decent chances, often kicking the ball away under little or no pressure. Gothenburg have been around a long time and punish such errors, cruising on to victory with plenty left in the tank for later.

As the second half starts, Niall drags us off to a corner of the pitch to start our warm-up. Call me old fashioned, but I've often wondered about the value of putting out cones and running a dozen different drills at full speed a few minutes before the game. I fully understand that the muscles of the body need to be warmed up, but the level and complexity of some of the routines seems a bit much. Coaches will tell you it's important that everyone gets their hands on the ball and that a game situation is simulated as much as possible; then they'll turn and scream at the players not to touch one another in case someone gets injured before the throw-in. I would feel an awful lot better if we were allowed to do a bit of jogging together and then continue our warm-ups individually. Being a fair bit older than some of the lads, it's hardly surprising that I feel the need to conserve energy, especially given the fact that there's a lot of football to be played over the course of the day. And besides, nothing lets you know you're in a game faster than getting a full back's elbow in the back of the head the first time the ball comes to you. No warm-up in the world can prepare you for that.

It's time. We take the field and pop a few shots at the posts as we wait for the ref to perform the coin toss. I jog around, kicking a few balls and chatting to our lads, giving a few final words of encouragement before we go into battle. As I jog I notice that one of the Malmö lads is wearing pink shorts; it turns out Brian Boyd is combining the first round of the championship with his stag weekend. I don't know why, but it puts me off. Then Malmö go into a huddle and break out of it shouting 'One, two, three — Malmö!' and that irritates me even more.

Niall gets us together and gives us a final talking to. He talks about Malmö and their huddle and their shouting and tells us it's all only hot air. He's seen teams like this before and he knows how to get at them. Don't get drawn into a fight with them. Keep the ball, play it short and move all the time. Controlled aggression. We have the players, and if we want to we can go out and win this game. There is no huddle, no big shout. The circle breaks and the subs head back to the sideline as the 11 starting players take up their positions, grim determination etched on their faces.

John Kelleher tosses the coin and it's game time. Colin lines up beside me up front as the lads go to the throw-in. This is it. It has been a year in the making, thousands of emails and hundreds of phone calls, dozens of training sessions and miles and miles of travels. The Stockholm Gaels are about to become a championship team.

We don't start well. We try the same set play as before and again we lose the throw-in, and we're on the back foot straight away. Niall was right. Championship football is a step up, and it's noticeable from the off. The ball moves quicker, the hits are bigger and it all seems to flash by in a flurry of arms and legs. We struggle with our passing game; as it is based on so many short passes, there are plenty of opportunities for things to go wrong, and in the beginning they do. Passes don't find their targets and we find ourselves struggling. I go for the first ball played in to me, low and hard just as I like it. The bang in the back of the head from the full back duly comes, and the ball breaks harmlessly away from me. But I've waited too long for this chance to show I'm not a coward any more, so I get up and get on with it: no calls to the ref, not a word to my marker. This is one game where I won't be backing down.

Colin and I find the routes to one another blocked as we try to eke out a few chances, and the few points that are put on the board by either side are scrappy, stolen more than scored. There's a nervousness in both teams' play. Malmö have obviously heard about the demolition job we did on Gothenburg and don't fancy being on the receiving end of a similar beating. We're an unknown quantity: we know we have plenty of skill and great finishers, but do we have the strength and the stamina needed? The two teams continue probing, asking each other the hard questions. Then disaster strikes.

Kevin Carroll had been doing his usual sterling job of playing all the positions across the back at once. His controlled running and awareness of how the play is developing allows him to pop up at just the right time to help out his defence, and he comes away with the ball. A quick exchange of passes and he is off up the sideline, only for his progress to be stopped by a very heavy challenge. He flies out over the sideline and is very slow to get up — too slow. Niall Balfe comes running across the pitch with his red bib on. Kevin is clutching the back of his leg. It looks like his hamstring is gone. 'Ach, it'll be all right lads. A bit of rest and I'll be back.' But we can see in his eyes he doesn't believe it. He's fucked. And without him, we're fucked.

Colin signals to Liam Kennedy to get stripped and get on the pitch as he and Niall start the unenviable task of reshuffling the pack so early in the game. Colin drops out to midfield as Liam joins me up front, with Niall taking Kevin's place beside Ken in the half back line. It doesn't feel like a total disaster, but having a front two with a combined age of over 85 is going to mean some changes to the way we play. We are going to have to run very hard for a very long time if we are to get anything out of this game.

Malmö sense the confusion and go about picking us off, pegging over a couple of scores with Brian in his pink shorts covering the ground and dictating the play, but we fight back hard and all of a sudden the running game starts to click. With Niall Scullion coming from deep and Colin getting on the ball more in the midfield, we start to open them up a little bit and force them back. Now the Sundbyberg Express is running on time and he and Mark O'Kane are cleaning up at the back, first to every ball, taking it cleanly and giving us a platform to build on the break. The ball comes into the midfield where Niall can run on to it, and things are starting to happen. Liam and I are coming out to receive the ball, then popping it back to the runner coming off our shoulder for a shot at goal. We get to half-time, shaken by the loss of our captain so early in the day but with our confidence somewhat restored.

All that goes out the window when disaster strikes again. Right from the throw-in we try our clear-out move again and once again it comes to nothing. We're still finding our feet in the second half when Malmö hit us with a sucker-punch goal and the wind is knocked out of us. I'm too far away to see exactly what happened, but all I could see was a lot of black jerseys standing still as the green and gold of Malmö ran around them to fire the ball home. Everything we talked about doing at half-time, about turning our dominance into scores and building up a lead, is all out the window. For the first time we are behind in a game and the next ten minutes would tell us more about our team and our character than we wanted to know. As Liam placed the ball on the tee for the kick-out, I shouted back down the field. 'You know what you have to do, fellas. You know what you have to do.' We could either roll over and give up, or we could roll up our sleeves and fight. As I turn and walk back towards the Malmö goal, the anger and frustration starts to bubble up inside me. I've seen very little ball and not had a single look at the posts in the first half, while Malmö are going around slapping each other on the back in front of me like they'd organised a kick-about for that fucker in his pink shorts on his stag do. They don't have to take the game seriously, and they don't have to take us seriously. I'm not having it. I take one last look back at our lads. The heads are shaking, but they never go down. I think to myself this one isn't over by a long shot.

Somehow in trying too hard to win it, we lost control of the kick-out and almost let Malmö in again, but an errant pass from them averts the danger and Niall drops back to pick it up. He looks up the field, looking to play a strategic clearance, but it's not on so he takes the short option to Declan instead. Declan finds Colin inside him and instantly the pace goes up a gear. Colin has seen Nigel make a move into some open space on the left, and he has already decided where he's going to put the ball before he's even caught it. Nigel advances and my man goes to close him down. Their defence is all over the shop as Nigel waits for the defender to advance on him before looping the ball over his head to me on the edge of the square. I've waited a long, long time for a chance like this, and there's only one way this is going to finish. I catch the ball and head straight for the goal.

Liam sees what I'm at and breaks off out towards the corner flag, pulling a defender with him and opening the path to goal. The goalkeeper quickly makes up his mind and rushes out to close me down as another defender drops in behind him to try to cover the line.

Since I started playing Gaelic football again, I have lost all the subtlety in my game. I got plenty of chances for goals against Gothenburg but wasted most of them by blasting the ball high and hard at the keeper from close range. The misses from that game flash through my mind as I take a bounce and advance, but I'm not worried about missing this one. This is my chance for revenge, my chance to put an end to all the slagging about the missed chances. The entire left side of the goal is wide open and in truth I won't need to hit it that hard, but I can't help myself. The anger and frustration at conceding a cheap goal at the other end boils over and I smash the ball as hard as I can. Neither the goalkeeper nor the defender on the line are anywhere close to being able to stop it. The net bulges and I let out a roar. We're back in the game.

The goal is cathartic, and now we're back to where we were at the end of the first half, but with a difference: we're getting the scores at the end of our moves. The ball is passed around like it was on a string, and forwards, midfielders and half backs are getting good looks at the posts. We pass and move fluidly as the points start to fly over from all angles, and Malmö can't seem to borrow the ball for a second. We score four unanswered points and all of a sudden our lead is getting bigger as the final whistle approaches. The game ends and we win by three points. We're off to a winning start! Not only that, we were dead and buried at the start of the second half, but we'd fought back.

For my own part, I was delighted. For once I didn't hide. I kept making the runs; I kept showing for the ball and taking the hits. And when the team needed something from me, I stepped up and provided it. I just hoped it wouldn't be the last time I would make such a contribution.

Next up was Oslo and a chance to build up a head of steam before the two tough games against Gothenburg and Copenhagen that would most likely have a big say in deciding who would contest the final. Oslo had struggled in their first game and we made the same mistake as many other teams did against us. We underestimated them from the start and struggled to establish any sort of a passing game. After the elation of the goal against Malmö, I was brought swiftly back down to earth; the young Norwegian lad marking me may not have been the most experienced Gaelic footballer on show, but he was young, quick and strong and could kick like a mule. Only once did I manage to get past him, only to shoot just wide.

Stockholm's class eventually told, with Ken Feely finally poking home a goal from his penalty rebound as the half forwards and midfielders added a flurry of points. The job was done, but it was by no means as easy as the scoreboard suggested, and with the sun appearing halfway through the game, this day was about to get tougher.

Meanwhile, big Freddie was making a name for himself in the Oslo midfield, and the lumbering giant finally broke the Norwegian side's scoring duck by pegging over a point against the Gaels with a well-taken effort. He was lucky to stay on the field in the second half as he kicked out at Mark O'Kane as the Derry man flew past him. Mark was sent sprawling in the dirt and by rights Freddie should have been sent to the line, if only to teach him a lesson. But given that Oslo weren't likely to get anything out of the game, he was allowed to stay on. Unfortunately, instead of learning his lesson and being a bit more careful on the pitch, his behaviour continued and would eventually result in him causing a serious injury in their home tournament. I can't help thinking that if he'd been sent off for the first offence he might have cleaned up his act.

Next up were our old friends from Gothenburg, and I was about to get reacquainted with the more bruising side of Billy Finn's nature. The addition of two extra teams in the championship had added a whole lot of spice and meant there was less room for slip-ups in any game. We knew Gothenburg would be gunning for us, looking for revenge for the drubbing they got in Stockholm, but we weren't about to play nice with anyone. With two victories under our belts, our sights were firmly set on reaching the final.

The last time we played them we had a much bigger squad at our disposal, and with Kevin Carroll now injured and his namesake John back at home in Stockholm with his pregnant wife, we weren't going to be knocking five or six goals past them this time. We started off well and built up a bit of a lead, but

Gothenburg weren't going to lie down. Liam got down to make a great save with his legs, but unfortunately the ball somehow squirmed through them and into the net. I had a great chance to make amends in the second half from almost exactly the same position as the Malmö goal, but this time I tried to place the ball between the keeper's legs and he blocked it. Luckily for us, Liam Kennedy was on hand to knock home the rebound as the oldest swingers in town started to make their presence felt in front of goal. Another victory chalked up — three games, three wins — and most teams were having difficulty finding a way to stop us.

Niall and Colin had done a great job from their positions on the pitch, coaching and cajoling, but the role of player-coach in Gaelic football is immensely demanding. Naturally, they were caught up in their own game, but we were having problems getting our substitutes into the game, and when we did get them in they weren't sure what it was they should be doing. The three victories were all well and good, but the physical effort of playing a quick-passing game was starting to take its toll as the afternoon got warmer. In between games our players sought out the shade of the dressing room or the minibus to stay out of the sun, and that was where the whispering started before our final group game against Copenhagen — were we already guaranteed a place in the final? And if we were, who would we meet there?

I could see Niall and Colin conferring at a corner of the pitch, and a few quick calculations proved that we were already there. But any suggestion of taking it easy in the last game was quickly dismissed. The result of our game against Copenhagen would have a direct bearing on whom we would meet in the final, and we owed it to the other teams to go out and give it our best shot. If Copenhagen were to beat us, we would meet them again in the final half an hour later. If not, we would meet Malmö. Given the choice of the two most physical sides in the tournament, I wasn't bothered. I didn't fancy playing either of them again.

We went out and gave our all against Copenhagen, but our tired minds and legs were finding it harder to deliver as the day wore on. We scrapped and scraped and battled our way through to a victory by six points to three. It wasn't pretty but it was effective. In our first tournament we had gone out and won every game. Now, all that was left was the final against a Malmö side hungry for revenge.

The Swedish girls played an exhibition against their Danish counterparts as we tried to shake the tiredness from our weary limbs for one last effort. I take over the filming duties as the girls go through their paces, and it's pretty obvious how Anna managed to be so successful on the Asian ladies' scene as she is one of the stand-out players on show. Tracey Sweeney's first competitive outing as a Gaelic footballer might have ended in defeat, but she seemed to enjoy every minute of it, as did another Swede, Maria Bejbrant. Maria was cornered by Anna one night in the Liffey and convinced to come along to training, and when she showed up she was a revelation. A talented soccer player, she clearly had an eye for ball sports and she picked up the basics right away, making fantastic progress in her first year. Family commitments meant she couldn't make it to too many tournaments, but when she did put the shirt on she was one of the most effective players we had. The game ended in a defeat for the Swedish side, but the fact that they managed to get two teams together was a triumph in itself.

As the lads prepared for the final, Niall's advice was simple: we've beaten these guys already today. Now all we have to do is go out there and do it again. But it wasn't going to be that easy. Malmö had seen us up close and watched us carefully during the day. They had a plan for the final and they were going to do their utmost to stop us.

The final was to be a grandstand affair. The Copenhagen club had set up a bar at the side of the pitch, with draught Carlsberg on sale, and now that Copenhagen, Gothenburg and Oslo would have no more games to play, the bartender was to join the referee as the busiest man in the parish that afternoon. All manner of benches were pulled from the dressing rooms outside to the sunshine on the sidelines as preparations were made for the first regional final of the year.

All the games we played that day were physical, but the final was to be the most demanding of them all. Whereas we had the beating of Malmö when it came to skill and speed, they were bigger and stronger than us, and as the day wore on they showed themselves to be the fittest team at the tournament too. They'd also done their homework, and it was obvious from the beginning that they saw Niall and Colin as the danger men and they wanted to stop them at all costs. From the throw-in, heavy challenges were administered every time either of them got on the ball. The Malmö players were careful not to foul them within shooting range for our free-taker Scullion, so often all we got was a free from too far out — if we got a free at all. The ref had continued to let the rough stuff go throughout the day, and given that Freddie from Oslo had stayed on the pitch despite kicking out at Mark, we knew we couldn't expect too many favours from him on that front.

Liam and I were almost completely starved of ball as our attacks were either broken up or our attackers brought down a safe distance from goal before they could play us in. We darted all over the forward line in an effort to make space for ourselves, but having given everything they had in winning the previous four matches, the lads simply couldn't get the ball up to us.

As clever as the Malmö lads were, we were getting stupid as the heat and lack of oxygen took their toll. Every time we made a silly foul in our own half, Malmö's place kicker Martin Long would saunter up and claim the ball. The Galway man would place the ball carefully on the ground before going through his kicking routine. The end result was inevitably that he split the posts every time. So in giving away frees we were simply handing scores to them. Add to that the time taken for each kick and the advantage was almost doubled as he racked up the scores whilst running down the clock, leaving us less and less time to retaliate. Martin is a lovely fella, but after that performance I didn't care if I never saw him again.

It was a war of attrition, and Malmö won it 0-6 to 0-3. I was still running as the final whistle blew, looking for one more chance to belt home an equalising goal and take the game to extra time, to finish the fairytale that had started a few months previously, but we would have to wait for that.

Our lads gathered in a tired circle and sat on the ground as the delirious Malmö players danced around and celebrated their victory.

'Look at them, lads. Look at them,' I said. 'Remember this feeling. And never let it happen again.'

Chapter 8 ~
| THE WEIGHT

The great thing about sport is that as long as you continue to play, there is always another chance, another game, another shot at redemption. I won't forget the final defeat to Malmö in a hurry — I doubt I'll ever forget it all — but thankfully we only had to wait a month for our shot at revenge. And with the next tournament taking place in Malmö, what a shot it would be. From the final whistle in Copenhagen, I had been looking forward to it.

That final whistle in Copenhagen signalled the start of a party for Malmö but only bitter disappointment for us. We trudged back to the car and the minibus, beaten, dirty and sweaty, worn out from the day's exertions. We had poured everything we had into the day and it wasn't enough. We came up short.

I felt most sympathy for Kevin Carroll, whose participation was ended in the first few minutes of the game by his injury. No matter what team sport I turn my hand to, I always seem to end up playing with teams far above my own level, which means I spend a lot of time on the bench. It must have been dreadful for Kevin to stand there all afternoon, shuttling over and back with the water bottles and a few words of advice, when what he really wanted was to be out there with the lads giving his all. There was a personal cost as well. With two young children at home, it was a huge sacrifice for both him and his wife Hannah to allow him to disappear off for the weekend to play football, not least in terms of the expense and the amount of time he would spend away from them. To have it all cut short after just a few minutes of playing time seemed unnecessarily cruel.

There was sympathy too for some of the lads on the substitutes' bench, who probably should have been utilised a lot more than they were. Barry Quinn and Niall Balfe had developed into capable forwards and young Viktor Widblom, the only Swede in the squad, was young, quick, strong and an excellent man marker. We really should have done better in terms of using them to close out games and to allow some of the other players to get some well-needed rest. But when everyone involved in coaching the team is actually playing themselves, the situation for those on the sidelines gets quickly forgotten. Having not seen too much ball myself as the day went on, I could empathise with their feeling of frustration. There's nothing like the feeling that, even though the final was lost, you still had something left in the tank. The lads on the line probably looked at those weary players on the pitch and thought they could do at least as well, if not better. Managing our playing resources was something we would have to work on, and it was probably the most valuable lesson to take from the day.

With all the kit and players back on board the bus, we returned to the hostel to have a shower before the teams got together for the dinner and the prize-giving ceremony that evening. To make it easier to take part in such tournaments, the host club is usually obliged to organise packed lunches during the day and an evening meal for everyone taking part. Indeed, this being the GAA, tournament rules state exactly what is to be included in the packed lunches. The cost of these meals is included in the registration fee that each player pays to take part. I had no interest in either the dinner or the prize-giving. The Champions League final was on that night and in a football-mad country like Denmark, the pub was bound to be packed.

As I sat in to the driver's seat of the minibus, still in my football kit, my mood turned from disappointment to defiance. Sure, we had been beaten in the final, but we felt justified in thinking we were the better football team on the day. Malmö had played well and adjusted their tactics after being beaten in the group game, but ultimately we ran out of steam. If we had been able to keep going at the pace we started no one could have lived with us.

We eventually gathered ourselves and made our way to the Globe pub. Given the choice, Copenhagen is probably the only other city in Scandinavia I'd live in and I'd visited it many times before today, but the Globe was in a part of town I wasn't familiar with, so it took us an age to get there. By the time we arrived, we were all starving and looking forward to whatever food had been laid on for us. The day then went from bad to worse. As we approached the bar where the food was being served and caught the first smell of the massive pot of stew bubbling away on a hotplate, the staff whipped it away, telling us we had arrived too late and they were no longer serving food.

For once I appreciated the up-front nature of the Danes as I gave the barmaid an earful. If she wanted to take the food away that was fine by me. All she had to do was refund the money to any of my players who hadn't yet been fed. They had paid for their food as part of the registration fee, and I was going to make damn sure they were going to get it. 'I don't have the authority to give refunds,' came the reply, as the cracks started to show. 'Maybe not, but you seem to have the authority to take away food that's already been paid for,' I thundered back. The pot was grudgingly replaced on the hotplate and a basket of fresh bread dumped beside it. Famished, some of the lads had already left to see if they could find a fast-food joint, but those that stayed behind finally got fed.

The word went around that the presentations were due to take place, and we crammed into a tiny room at the front of the pub. It was the last place on earth I wanted to be, but not to show up would have seemed like sour grapes on our part, and despite the row over the food I wasn't that unhappy. We had won four of our five games and played some tremendous football on the day, and everything we had done we had done in a sporting manner. True, I would have been happier if we had won the final, but I couldn't be more proud of what our club and our team had achieved in such a short space of time.

The lads from Copenhagen made some great speeches; many of them have been active in European GAA for many years and it was great to see how much they enjoyed the expansion of the tournament, even if their own club hadn't made the final. Despite us losing the final, Anna Rönngård was named player of the game for the ladies' exhibition match, so we wouldn't be going home empty handed after all. Despite awarding the player of the tournament award to a Polish lad from their own team, they singled out our own Colin Courtney for special praise. No doubt Colin enjoyed that, but I'd say he would have traded all the praise for the winner's trophy that Malmö were about to receive.

The speeches over, the trophy was presented to the Malmö captain, flanked by Brian the bridegroom, who was now sporting a fetching dress and a flower in his hair. Their victory speech was short and sweet and full of encouragement for the Oslo lads who had battled so hard for little reward all day. That part of the speech struck a chord with me. It is traditional in sporting victory speeches to make some reference to your opponent when receiving a trophy, but not once did the Malmö captain mention us in his acceptance speech. That was enough for me.

The Malmö players were applauded and we left the stuffy

room. As predicted, the pub was now packed and the bar staff were chasing people who had come in just to watch the football but hadn't bought a drink. There was little chat or banter around the table; the lads were simply worn out after the day, and the disappointment of losing hung like a cloud over them. I stuck around for the Champions League final, but between the brutal football being offered up by Inter and Bayern Munich and the Malmö victory speech, I'd had enough. A hundred minutes of football in the hot sunshine had taken their toll, and I was exhausted. I'd seen enough trophy presentations for one day. As soon as the final whistle went, I grabbed Kevin Carroll and we jumped in a taxi back to the hostel on the outskirts of town.

A short time later Kev was performing his reverse Lazarus act on the top bunk again, sound asleep and dead to the world in his bed without so much as a peep out of him, as I lay quietly fuming on the bunk below. I began planning for our revenge.

Nursing the wounds of the day before, we checked out of the hostel early the next morning. Given our defeat in the final, no one wanted to hang around the scene of the crime any longer than was necessary, and when reports got out about the Sundbyberg Express sleepwalking naked through the halls of the hostel, we decided not to hang around for the inquest. A quick breakfast was had and the rooms were emptied and cleaned as the vehicles were loaded up again for the long trip home. The only silver lining on the long journey was a text message received from Ronan, who promised us all a pint at the Dub on our return. This little gesture was enough to put our defeat into perspective. The lads back home thought we'd done a great job reaching the finals, so either we were a brilliant side that fell just short, or they didn't think much of our chances in the first place. I decided to go with the former.

Colin and the lads piled into the car. The last thing I saw as they pulled out of the car park was Declan's massive frame squashed up against the window in the back of the car, slightly hung over and with a look of utter misery etched on his face.

Compared to the boisterous craic and drinking games of the journey down, it was a subdued bus on the way home and the journey seemed to take forever. I was the only driver insured on the minibus and there was no way I was going to risk letting anyone else take over the driving duties, even for a short distance. Having driven to Denmark on my own several times before, I was glad of the company that the others provided, but as the fatigue from the weekend kicked in and the realisation dawned that tomorrow was going to be a working day for most of us, one by one the passengers in the back drifted off to sleep. My rearview mirror was soon filled with sleeping heads. I struggled to get RTÉ radio on my smartphone to listen to the afternoon's hurling as we made our way back.

The mood got a little better as we arrived back at the Dubliner. Since the dawn of the internet and the advent of social media, the world has become a much smaller place, and we had been able to keep everyone back in Stockholm and Ireland updated about our progress via Facebook and sms. The staff and customers in the Dubliner and the Liffey had been able to keep an eye on us throughout the day, posting messages of encouragement and urging us on, and a few of them were still in the pub on the Sunday evening when we arrived. It was a bizarre feeling: they were all proud of us and our achievement in getting to the final, but those of us who had been there knew just how close we had come to winning the whole thing at the first attempt. Ronan was as good as his word and most of the lads stayed around for a drink at the Dub before heading off home to lick their wounds. The next round was only a few weeks away and there was no time to waste.

Back in Stockholm the training is stepped up a notch. Even without seeing the footage that we have filmed from all the

Copenhagen games, there was no doubt about the level of skill we had in our team. But we know we need to be fitter and stronger if we are to go the extra mile and start winning tournaments outright.

In the beginning I had hoped we weren't going to have to waste too much time and effort on the fitness aspect, and proposed that each player be responsible for his or her own fitness. I wanted to play as much football as possible in the limited time available to us, and besides, most of the players seemed to have another couple of sports or activities that would take care of that aspect. Karl Lambert — the Sundbyberg Express — was a good example. Karl is no stranger to a few beers and a big dinner, but he is also one of the fittest people I've ever met, and his enthusiasm for training is infectious. An avid distance runner, he and Keith Hearne regularly went on long training runs together and they took part in marathons and half-marathons with seeming ease. When not out pounding the pavements Karl is to be found in the gym pumping iron and preparing for his next challenge.

To me it seemed better to use the time we had together as a team to work on ball skills, especially for the less-experienced players and indeed the Swedes and other nationalities who were joining us for the first time. This made even more sense, given the talented players like Colin, Niall, Mark and Declan we had to learn from.

But our coach Niall is the boss and he rightly included a strong element of physical training in his sessions. For some time he and Colin have been trying to persuade Phil Cahill, a Meath man with inter-county experience and a fanatical interest in fitness, to join us as a coach, and Phil starts to show up more and more at our sessions. Phil's quiet, methodical way of setting up the sessions leaves nothing to chance, and even when the ball is introduced to a drill there's usually an underlying aspect of strength, fitness or balance that he is trying to develop or improve. The lads might be great marathon runners, but the kind of fitness and strength used for running marathons is totally different to what is needed to play 100 minutes of Gaelic football in a day, which not even the top inter-county players back home are asked to do.

The benefits of having Phil are twofold: he has hundreds of exercises and drills that are specifically designed to help and improve the Gaelic footballer, and his presence also allows Niall and Colin to concentrate on their own fitness and strength training. Rather than going around and making sure everyone else is doing everything right, they can let Phil run the show and put the work in themselves, getting the benefit of it at the tournaments. The concept of the player-manager is almost unheard of in top-level Gaelic football, and given the issues we've had with getting the team fit and managing it during games, it soon becomes apparent to us why this is so.

As the weather improves and the evenings get longer, the Wednesday sessions start to become more and more about building up core fitness, with Sundays at Östermalms IP more dedicated to ball work. We always try to get a game in at the end of every session — we still want to be primarily a football team, not a bunch of iron men — but the football part is something that comes naturally to many of us, whereas the fitness isn't. The sessions often extend beyond the allotted times, with bodies worked to the point of exhaustion out on the training field in the hope of staving off that feeling for as long as possible when the next tournament comes around.

The GAA is famously an amateur association, with no player receiving payment for taking part, but the higher up you go and the more you want to succeed, the more a professional attitude to training is required. The discipline required extends to the pub and the kitchen too, as refuelling a body trying to achieve maximum performance is at least as important as exercising it. Trying to balance all this with a working and family life is a massive challenge for anyone who takes the game seriously at any level.

Breaking my arm the previous summer had given me a whole new perspective on how I train myself. Whilst in the cast, the muscles in my arm had basically withered away, and when the cast was finally cut off after almost six weeks, it unveiled a pale mass of grey skin and bone. A physiotherapist showed me various exercises that would help improve my grip again over time, but an awful lot more would need to be done. Despite being over six foot tall I had never been the dominant physical presence on the football field or the basketball court that I felt I could have been. So when it came to rehabilitating my arm, I decided I was going to go in the other direction and put on as much muscle as I could. Mentally I knew I would always beat myself up over my performances, but this wouldn't be going on for very much longer. There's a limit to what the body can take and approaching 40 I wasn't sure I would be able to keep it up for too many years more. But I was determined to get as strong as I possibly could for the remainder of the season. I'd shown down in Copenhagen that I wasn't going to back down any more. Now it was time to ensure that I wasn't going to get pushed over either. But where do you start?

Despite regular attendance at the gym I'd never seen any progress whatsoever in terms of muscle development from using weights. Granted, the knee problem and pain that had curtailed my basketball career had disappeared once I got a proper programme of weight training to strengthen up the muscles around it, but other than that I'd felt that I'd pumped a whole lot of iron for little or no return. I didn't want to go back to the gym and do what I'd always done, because the results would be the same. It was time to consult with the experts.

To those who do it regularly, lifting weights is a cross between an addiction and a religion. Every single dedicated gym enthusiast seems to believe that theirs is the one shining truth and everything else is a waste of time. Some will tell you not to bother with machines, as by isolating muscles you are ignoring the supporting muscles around them, and that lifting free weights works all the required muscles in tandem. Others will say that only by targeting specific muscles can you make them obey your demands. There are still others who think it's heresy to enter a gym at all, and that the resistance provided by your own bodyweight is all you need. Personally I don't care about the method. All I want to know is will it make me strong enough to hold off Aidan O'Reilly, otherwise known as Ginge, the granite-hard Malmö full back, the next time we meet.

Shortly after the cast came off, I made the mistake of consulting with more than one person about what I should do in the gym to become the strongest footballer I could be. Of course they gave me two programmes which more or less contradicted each other on every point — all very well motivated and explained but the complete opposites of one another. My friend Rodrigo, a top-class soccer coach, had advised a lot of balance training and using small weights to build up the explosive power he saw as being necessary for Gaelic football, whereas the resident expert in the gym prescribed lifting heavy weights to build up muscle mass and raw strength. Having spent over ten years adapting to Sweden's consensus society, I decided both of them were right and created a programme of my own.

I started by only using the Smith machine, which is basically a bar on a set of rails. You put the weights on either side of the bar and then lift them using various muscles. For instance, by putting the bar across the back of your shoulders you can work the big leg muscles by doing squats, or you can choose to work the muscles in your chest by lying on a bench and raising the bar repeatedly. To these basic exercises, I added and subtracted others to work on the areas I felt needed developing, using a combination of free weights and machines. Judging by the stiffness and pain on my rest days, I must have been doing something right.

Creating such a programme is not really to be recommended and I'd be the first to admit that I know little or nothing about physiology compared to the two guys who had given me programmes. As an amateur you also run the risk of chopping and changing your routine and never giving it a fair chance to take effect. Technique is also important, and lifting the right weight in the wrong way is not only pointless but it can also be dangerous. But my old indiscipline with regard to training kicked in. I had a programme that took about 40 minutes in the gym every second day, which was about the amount of time I was prepared to invest in it.

Of course all the weights and training in the world won't make the blindest bit of difference if you don't eat properly, so that was another area that needed a total overhaul. Sport and life in general are full of ridiculous fad diets that are supposed to give you a Baywatch body from eating nothing but mango fruit, and sorting out the truth from the myth about food and supplements is a minefield. After plenty of reading and canvassing of opinions I decided to take a protein supplement and Creatine to see if it could help me build the muscle I needed to hold Ginge and Freddie at bay. I'd seen what it had done for the likes of the Irish rugby team, and though I had little chance of standing in Lansdowne Road singing 'Ireland's Call' as anything other than a supporter, I figured there must be something behind these supplements so I'd give them a try.

As a rule, these supplements taste horrible. There's a reason that nature wraps up protein and carbohydrates in other forms for human beings to eat as food. In their raw state they taste absolutely manky. Sometimes it depends on the brand, but having tried most of the varieties available on the market, the best thing to do is find one that doesn't make you gag or vomit and stick to it. It's not likely to get any better.

But man cannot live on protein powder and vitamin supplements alone, and I certainly can't feed it to the kids. Whatever about supplements, they are no substitute for a proper diet of real food and, like training, it takes time and discipline in the kitchen to get the right results. Out went fatty and sugary foods like sweets and cakes, and takeaways were only acceptable in serious emergencies. It felt like I was eating constantly once I started the weight-training programme. Kids in Sweden get a hot lunch in school, and the younger ones can even eat their breakfast at daycare, so all that was left was to arrange a wholesome dinner every day. In the meantime I was using the sickly protein shakes directly after training and as a snack, together with nuts, berries and fruit to keep me going between meals.

One of the biggest difficulties in gaining and maintaining muscle and fitness is the constant eating. It's hard to actually get in as many calories as you need. Anyone who wants to see how much food a serious athlete goes through need only watch an ice hockey team eat lunch. I've never seen anything like the amount of food those guys can put away in a single sitting, and they repeat this feat several times a day. It's scary, but now I was beginning to understand why and where it all went.

I gave up drinking a few years ago after that fantastic day out on the beer for St Patrick's Day — or rather after the massive hangover that followed it. I usually say that that was the day Seán Beatty finally broke me, but in truth I had been thinking about knocking it on the head for a while. For years I had worked in restaurants and nightclubs with music, and when I worked in marketing I started to spend my time on the other side of the bar. Regardless of which side you're on, if you're young and in that environment there is a tendency to drink too much and have the craic. But now I had two small children, and never being much of a morning person to begin with, hangovers could no longer be enjoyed or endured. I'm still threatening to go on a bender the day my two little girls move out of the family home, but I'd say by that point a bender for me will last about half an hour or two beers before I'm sent home in disgrace, never to be allowed back in the pub again.

When it comes to drink, I'm conscious of the problems it can cause in the club as well. A lot of our players are young fellas in their twenties, so it's only natural they are out late on a Friday and Saturday night drinking beer and chasing a bit of romance. I'd be more worried about them if they weren't. Needless to say some of them didn't exactly cover themselves in glory on certain Sundays as they arrived to training in the clothes they went out in the night before. We've had a lot of volunteers for goalkeeping duties on those days.

I'm not alone in the club in not drinking either; Niall is another one who has foresworn the apparent joys of alcohol. I don't think he's ever mentioned why he doesn't drink and I doubt I would ever ask him. Often on our travels to tournaments lads would ask us, 'Do you not find it difficult not drinking in this situation?' Our answer is usually the same: you'd be surprised how easy it is *not* to do something. Besides we know the state they will find themselves in the next morning when we're checking out and heading off on the long drive home.

It may also seem weird that two non-drinkers have such leading roles in a sporting organisation sponsored by two pubs, but that sits comfortably with us too. Irish pubs abroad are about so much more than just alcohol. They are the meeting places for our community and without their involvement the GAA clubs wouldn't have a chance of surviving. They are a primary source of the two things we need more than anything else — players and money.

It must also be pointed out that given his love of Gaelic games and his current status as a single man, Niall spent many happy hours over the weekends this past summer in the Dubliner or the Liffey, eating his meals there and watching as the All-Ireland Gaelic football and hurling championships unfolded. And if the Dublin hurlers or footballers were on TV, the two noisiest characters in the whole place were usually the two most sober as I sat on the stool beside him and argued loudly — and often ignorantly — with my blue-tinted glasses about the prospects for the Dublin footballers or hurlers this year.

Given the surge of interest in the club and our near-miss in the final in Copenhagen, what was originally supposed to be a friendly game between the two pubs started to take on a greater significance. We had at first penned in the game as a way of saying thanks to the two pubs for their sponsorship, and the buzz created around it would no doubt lead to a few beers being had in both establishments. The idea was that the squad hoping to travel to the next round of the championship in Malmö would be split in two and complemented by staff from the pubs and others who, for one reason or another, couldn't normally travel with us.

It was also a chance to get the wives, girlfriends and children together and get to know one another, if they didn't already. We had no problem taking credit for the great sacrifices we all made as players in terms of time and effort and money spent training and going to tournaments, but the sacrifices were also made by the partners we left behind to look after the children. Most of these relationships consisted of one Irish person and one Swede, so they had at least that in common to begin with. For the children, this was even more important. There aren't too many Irish people living in Sweden, so was important to get the few of them that are there together so that the children realise they are not alone.

One of the weird things about being Irish rather than some other nationality in Sweden is the language. Almost without exception, Swedes speak excellent English, so from the very beginning they have something of an advantage over us, at least until we learn Swedish. If you come from Argentina or Iran, you can use your mother tongue to your children safe in the knowledge that not too many people around you will understand what you are saying, and even if they do, there is a shared cultural background. But if I speak English to my children on the street or in a shop, I instantly feel everyone looking and listening to me. My wife, being a language teacher, insists that I only speak English with the kids so as not to confuse them, but given the choice between confusing them or being embarrassed at having a whole street full of people looking at me, I think I know which I'd rather do.

Then there is the language itself. Being surrounded by Swedish all day, it's often the case that this language develops quickest for the children and their English lags behind; after all, they usually only have one person speaking to them in English every day, and that person (me) might be at work for most of the day. So getting together in a mixed environment and having to switch from Swedish to English and back again depending on whom they are talking to brings out the best in their linguistic skills.

It's amazing to see how quickly the Irish-Swedish children click when they get together. It's like they understand that on some level they are not exactly like the other kids around them in school or daycare, but when they come into this environment they are at home. For the most part their Irish grannies and granddads still live in Ireland, whereas their friends from Turkey or Syria might have the whole family living close by here in Stockholm. For kids with two Swedish parents, the holidays might be spent in Mallorca or Thailand, but it's not unusual for a Swedish-Irish child to spend their summer holidays staring out at a rainy Limerick landscape dreaming of a beach somewhere in warmer climes.

Colin, Niall and I have decided it's time to get the next generation of Stockholm Gaels acquainted with Gaelic games, so we've invited all the families with young children to come down early for a training session for the kids. We've bought some miniature footballs and some pop-up goals, and in no time at all Niall Scullion has them hand passing the ball between one another like true Northern footballers. Despite the wide range of ages from 3 to 13 or so, the kids are more or less on the same level, having never played the game before. The older ones get the hang of it quicker and start to help the younger ones out, and much shrieking and laughter accompanies the chaotic game at the end.

Despite being still sidelined by his hamstring injury, Kevin Carroll has been up at the crack of dawn to improvise a set of goalposts for the challenge match between the Liffey and the Dubliner, and as the kids' session goes on he attaches wooden extensions to the soccer posts to make something resembling a Gaelic football goal. There is nothing more enjoyable for a full forward than playing with soccer goals; the extra width makes all the difference when shooting for goal.

Karl Stein from the Liffey is taking this game seriously and has brought out a number of lads from the kitchen and behind the bar to play. Of the two pubs the Liffey is undoubtedly the 'little brother' of the Dub, which has existed in Stockholm for over 15 years and is probably the best-known Irish watering hole in the country. But Karl is undeterred. Something of a marketing genius with a seemingly endless store of brilliant ideas, he has emptied the kitchen and the bar of staff and brought them all out with him to pose in front of the Liffey banner. Despite the friendly nature of the game, both publicans know there is prestige to be played for, and the needling starts as the players are split into the two teams.

This is also a chance to involve lads who wouldn't otherwise have an opportunity to play Gaelic football. The likes of 'Tall Paul' Finan from Galway and Mark O'Sullivan are heavily involved in soccer teams in the city and don't have the time or the energy to make the commitment to Gaelic football as well. This is a shame in Paul's case, as a big, aggressive guy like him would be worth his weight in gold against the more physical teams in Scandinavia. Don Corry will be joining us too, another great soccer player who has shared custody of his children. Occasionally reckless in the tackle, Don has an engine like no other and would run all day. Mark has also brought with him a young Swedish soccer player he has been coaching. Having only been shown the basics in the few minutes before the throw-in, the young lad showed himself to be an absolute natural and he gave an assured display as a full back in the 11-a-side game.

John Carroll was chosen to referee the game, and despite the high degree of respect that everyone has for him as a player, he got absolutely slated by everyone as soon as he blew the whistle. The Liffey streaked out to an early lead, but amid rumours of bribes to the referee the Dubliner clawed their way back into the game, helped in no small way by some dodgy decisions and the odd stroke of outrageous good fortune. The game ended after an hour with the Dub running out narrow winners, but the discussions were to continue long into the night. Ronan from the Dubliner had a couple of cases of beer with him which were unloaded after the final whistle and which only served to make the discussions longer and more intense.

Once again the Irish community turned out to watch the spectacle and though we didn't have as many spectators as we had at the Gothenburg game, the trend was still positive. All of a sudden people were meeting each other for the second or third time, and even more encouragingly I heard snatches of conversations where people were discussing what they did for a living and how they could maybe help one another in the future. One of those present took the opportunity to invite a few others to a trade show, and word was passed around about what playgrounds were popular hangouts for English-speaking parents, or what singers and bands were coming to town with a view to perhaps meeting up there.

The situation of the Irish community in Stockholm up to that point was by no means unique, but it does have certain characteristics that set it apart from other communities in Europe or around the world. One thing it has in common with them is that there are as many emigrant stories as there are emigrants. Sure, some of the elements such as love and job prospects might be the same, but every story of how a person came to live in a particular place and in a particular set of circumstances is different. Some have come with a girlfriend to try living here for a year or two, and ended up with a wife and children (sometimes the wife is not necessarily the same girl he came over with). Some are here long-term and speak the language, living in the suburbs or a posh downtown apartment, whilst others are here studying, doing research or on secondment for a big international company back in Dublin or London. Some had barely been out of the country before fate dumped them in Scandinavia one dark midwinter, whereas others had travelled the world before winding up here and had a mountain of experience to call on.

Like the myth that all Swedes look like a member of ABBA, there is a similar myth about how sociable the Irish are, and that the first thing we do when we land in a new country is head to the nearest Irish pub, sing a ballad or two, get drunk, and all of a sudden we're friends for life. The reality is nothing at all like that. The Swedes have a particular approach to drinking; they didn't even drink that much beer until the last 50 years or so. Prior to that Sweden was, along with Finland and Russia, a part of the vodka belt where home-distilled vodka was the tipple of choice.

Swedes were never known as social drinkers; they may not have drunk that often, but when they did they drank to get drunk. Going for a pint the way the Irish do was much less common, and even if it has become more accepted in the intervening years, there is still the old Lutheran mindset that anyone who drinks even small amounts regularly must be an alcoholic. It seems it's better to save up the week's ration until the weekend and then drink it as fast as possible before heading for a nightclub on a Saturday night.

Even if Irish people do have a natural meeting place in the pub, it is not to everybody's taste, and if you are looking to meet strangers and form lasting friendships during your stay in Sweden, maybe it's not the right place to start. It's not really the best place to bring children either, which rules out a lot of people. When I arrived here in 1999 the Irish pubs were mostly the preserve of the young lads in their early twenties and I met many of the lads that were now part of the club — Barry Quinn, Ronan, Jim Kelly. The problem for me was that as I was trying to set myself up in Sweden and find a job, I had neither the time nor the money to spend in Irish pubs. But there was simply nowhere else to run into them. Starting the Gaels finally gave us a way in which to meet each other, and even if we did spend plenty of afternoons and evenings in the pub, it wasn't the centre of the universe — the playing pitch was. At least now we had something to offer everyone, no matter what their background was or how long they would be staying in the country, and today was a shining example of what had been missing in the past.

For the club, the diversity of experience we have gathered together is as beneficial as it is dangerous. The communities back home offer a much more stable environment. People who have family ties to an area, who work and own homes there, aren't as mobile as a young couple on short-term contracts in a European city. The coaches and committee at our club are forever working in the knowledge that we could wake up one morning and half the club could have left town. Niall's employer could call him back to Ireland or the UK, and if and when the Irish Defence Forces finish their exercises with the Nordic Battle Group, we will lose two of the best players on the men's and women's teams. God forbid if Colin's company was ever to lose its contract with one of the Swedish banks. Not only would we lose the cornerstone of the forward line, we'd also lose Mark, Ken and Declan. Four of our starting 11 in most championship matches would be gone in one fell swoop.

As I look around the people gathered here in the aftermath of the game, I'm struck by the fragility of our situation. This should be something of a moment of triumph, to have 40 or 50 Irish people and their partners and children all gathered in the one place, but it only accentuates how precarious our position is. The likes of myself, Ronan and Karl Stein have been here for years. Our children were born here and no matter how much we might want to move back at some point in the future, we aren't likely to go anywhere any time soon. But we cannot keep this going alone. Mick O'Connell, the former head barman at the Dubliner who is now working in one of the English schools, is another who has been here for a very long time. His son Danny is a tremendous soccer player and would no doubt be a great asset if he learned to play Gaelic football. The thought strikes me that the future of the club lies not just with the likes of Mick and Danny and the rest of the Irish community here, but with people whose names we don't yet know. We will be dependent on the next generation of Irish emigrants forced to look to Scandinavia for work or who follow a sweetheart here. But one thing is certain: at some point somewhere along the line we will need to increase the involvement of the Swedes and others if the club is to survive.

The day is drawing to a close. Keith Hearne and his partner Malin had invited everyone back to a barbecue in their garden, so they rushed home directly after the game to get everything ready. The rest of us stayed on to gather up the kit and stow the improvised goalposts behind the dressing rooms for future use before heading off down the road to their house. I brought a gang of players back to my place to shower, and half an hour later we went around the corner to Keith's house. To make it easier to find he had hung his treasured Waterford jersey on the hedge outside, but he needn't have bothered. The garden was packed with people eating, drinking and talking in the early summer sunshine, and the Irish accents would have been hard to miss as you could hear them a mile off. We'd bought a couple of crates of beer and some wine from the club kitty, and it was one of the most enjoyable afternoons I have had during my time in Sweden. To think that we as a club had pulled together so many people from so many different backgrounds in such a short space of time was a source of great pride to us all. Slowly but surely the relationships that are the glue that bind a strong and vibrant community together were starting to form.

Chapter 9 ~

| NOT FADE AWAY

Whatever you want to achieve on the football pitch, you need to have stamina. Reaching the final of a Scandinavian championship tournament demands that the best players often have to play over 100 minutes of football in a single day, something which very few athletes are asked to do. Add to that the fact that the games are lightning quick, win-or-lose affairs with little room for error, and you can begin to understand the massive physical pressure the players are under. Like any long-distance relationship, our meetings with our fellow clubs in Scandinavia may be infrequent, but they are all the more intense for it.

With the snow long since melted, the bike is taken down to the repair shop for a once-over, and I have no doubt the old boy who runs it is ripping me off when I get the bill for the service. He'll soon be retiring and it seems he's eager to squeeze the last few quid out of his golden goose while he still can. Given the money I've paid to get it back on the road, I resolve to use it as much as I can.

I start to cycle the 12 kilometres into the office in downtown Stockholm every day, and in no time at all I can feel the difference as my aerobic fitness starts to improve dramatically. From there I start to make bigger diversions. Having made the move into journalism, I find myself having to attend press conferences at the national stadium or at some hotel around town, and the press officers have become accustomed to the sight of me chaining my bike to the railings before running up the stairs to put my Dictaphone on the table for an afternoon's work.

The gains made on the bike start to become apparent on the soccer and Gaelic football pitches too as I'm able to run harder for longer. I'm still lacking in speed, but then again I was never the quickest, and between the weights programme and the gym I'm starting to feel I might just be approaching the physical shape I feel I need to be in when we get to Malmö.

I also got some great help from two soccer-playing friends, Carl Thywissen and Thomas Frost. A Norwegian and a Dane respectively, both had played soccer at a very high level, Carl in Scotland and Thomas in Denmark, and they swore by neoprene 'warm pants' as a sure-fire way to avoid groin strains, hamstring pulls and other injuries. After a five-a-side game one night, they convinced me that these miracle shorts could soon cure the ongoing pain in my groin muscle. Once I got over the mental image of what 'warm pants' might be, I got on the internet and bought a pair. Made from the same material as is used to make scuba diving suits, they keep your muscles supported and warm and I can safely say that since I got them I haven't had a single moment's trouble with any of the 'old man' injuries mentioned above.

With all this endless and meticulous preparation, we were almost ready to take up the cudgels again. The disappointment at losing that final in Copenhagen hasn't gone away at all, but now for the first time I'm actually looking forward to the next tournament in Malmö and the chance for revenge.

Word of our success in Copenhagen has spread, and all of a sudden there are offers of help and promises of support coming in from all sides. Mark O'Sullivan, a former Cork City footballer and all-round sportsman, shows up to take a training session, coming up with yet more new drills that are a combination of pleasure and torture. Mark works a lot with the youth of Stockholm and has a few great tips on how to access state funding for sport. No matter where it comes from, money is always welcome.

More and more players start to turn up to our training sessions on Sundays and Wednesdays, and the membership fees are flooding in from those who were biding their time, making sure this wasn't just some flash-in-the-pan outfit that was here for the beer and would be gone in no time having pocketed their membership fees.

The journalists are back on our trail again. The good friends we made with the Hansson story are following our progress from the Irish sports desks, and quite a few messages of encouragement drop into our inbox. Money is still pretty tight, but the wider we cast our net, the more doors we have to knock on. Regardless of how much we have in the kitty, the Copenhagen tournament has proved to many that this is now very much a viable club with a future, not least ourselves.

It's not so long since we were worrying about getting enough players together to play against Gothenburg in a friendly back in April; now we find ourselves with a totally different and much more sensitive problem. The rules for European regional competitions say that we can only name a squad of 18 players for each tournament and a team of 15 players for each game, but judging by the expressions of interest we're going to have way more than that travelling to Malmö. A lovely problem for a young club to have, but a problem all the same. Who do you leave out?

For most clubs back in Ireland the answer is pretty straightforward. You take your best team to the tournament and then you try to win every game and bring back the trophy. But we are not most clubs and our circumstances are very different from those back home. After all, what is one trophy worth to us if in winning it we alienate the very players on whom the future depends?

First, there are those who were there from the very beginning and who travelled to the first tournament. In certain cases they have invested a lot of time and money in the club and have got very little in return. Now when other supposedly 'better' players come along, are they supposed to step aside? I know I wouldn't be happy if that were the case, no matter how much I want the club and the team to succeed. This in particular will be a problem for the Malmö tournament. John Carroll, who alongside Colin is probably the most naturally gifted footballer we have, is available to travel, as is his neighbour from Cabra, Sean Beatty. Sean is a great character, a tremendous athlete who possesses a unique ability to read the game whether it be soccer, Gaelic football or any other ball sport. His fitness and intelligence mean that his inclusion in the squad will threaten more than one of us as he can play in virtually any position. If he travels there is little doubt he will end up getting playing time at the expense of someone else. My neighbour, marathon man Keith Hearne, would also be available and though more a hurler than a footballer, with his smart play and incomparable stamina he is going to fit right in somewhere too, again taking playing time off someone else.

The biggest threat to me personally would be Ciarán O'Reilly from Cavan. Ciarán is a big, powerful, direct forward, well able to look after himself and hard to stop once he gets up a head of steam. He replaced me against Gothenburg and gave a towering display which threw my misses in front of goal into sharp relief. It says a lot about how gifted a player Ciarán is that I could score 2-2 and still be in his shadow. If he is travelling to Malmö, then my place in the starting line-up is in serious doubt.

Non-Irish clubs also have to wrestle with an issue that few if any clubs at home ever need to worry about. We have to manage new adult players coming into our clubs and nurture them accordingly. These adults are often foreigners who have no history in or knowledge of the game but who are often in decent physical shape and have reached the top in other sports. Our ladies' captain Anna is an excellent example of this. More importantly they represent the future of our clubs, and if we are to grow Gaelic games beyond our own island we need to not only welcome them into our clubs but to fully integrate them and provide them with competitive action so that they can play a full part in our development. Being adults, they don't have the time or the patience to wait around for years for this to happen, so we have to do our best to train them up and get them in there as quickly as we can. But balancing that with our own goals of winning games and tournaments is a hard act. For them and us it's a simple trade-off: they want to learn and play the game, and if we don't let them do it they'll go back to playing soccer or whatever else. For us, we need them to continue, but we also need to keep winning, because nothing attracts players and investment like a winning team. If anyone has come up with a formula for solving this problem, they haven't shared it with me.

Take the example of James Guanci in our own club. Born in America, James was probably our most improved player during the spring when he added the basic skills of Gaelic football to his imposing soldier's frame. He marked me regularly in our training games during that period and in the beginning I thought it would be boring for me and that someone with my experience and knowledge would give him the runaround — another massive underestimation on my part. It was amazing to see how he developed into a fine footballer over the course of just a few short weeks. By the time the late summer internal tournament came around, I dreaded meeting him.

But at the same time, if he makes the 18-man squad for the Malmö tournament, there is a good chance he will see a very limited amount of game time; unless we have a number of injuries, he's going to spend a lot of his time on the bench down in Malmö. Not only do we want revenge for the final defeat in Copenhagen, we know it is within our grasp. Giving James game time in that situation might represent an unacceptable risk on our part. It's a delicate matter, but it has to be dealt with all the same.

With more and more administration and planning to be done, I'm now totally out of the loop in terms of team selection. A small part of me would like to be involved, if only to know precisely what I can expect of myself when it comes to playing time and what role I would be expected to perform. But I haven't got the time or the energy to discuss it. The problem of how to handle everyone's expectations around Malmö is an issue not just for the coaches but for the whole club, and long, arduous and sensitive discussions take place over a period of ten days before it is decided that a squad for Malmö will need to be selected from those willing to travel. The decision will be emailed out to everyone at the same time — not a perfect solution by any means, but like I say, if there's a better one, I haven't heard it.

Phil Cahill won't be making the trip this time, so Niall has to hold on to the role of head coach, and as such he's the one that has to bite the bullet and send the mail informing everyone about the squad. Again, the role of the player-coach is a thankless one. There is very little chance he is going to drop himself to the bench at any point (nor should he, given that he is one of the best footballers in Scandinavia), so it will be very easy to point the finger and criticise. Anyone outside the squad will find plenty to say about whoever dropped them, whether they are playing or not. Then there is always the opportunity for anyone who didn't make the cut to travel down and play for another club as the other clubs don't have anywhere near the number of players we have. Few seem to want to accept this invitation.

Aside from the lads who went to Copenhagen, Keith, James,

John Carroll and Seán Beatty will be joining us, as will Cork man Colin Cotter. Colin is a tigerish little player who is always a bonus to have in the side, but given that he has joint custody of his daughter he is not at liberty to travel as freely as he might like. Given how we ran out of legs in Copenhagen, we'll have to make much better use of the subs available to us in Malmö, and Colin's playing style should fit right in.

Sometimes I wish this was a professional club where we had loads of money and could just go ahead and make the travel arrangements for everybody, but that day is probably still a long way off. With the limited resources we have available and the fact that everyone must contribute to their travel and accommodation, we can only offer them options, not solutions. I'm starting to suspect that Colin Courtney has some sort of bizarre deal with his partner Linn regarding their car, because once again he volunteers to transport some of the team to the tournament. The fact that Colin can bring his own car and that a lot of the guys in the team work with him at one of the banks in the middle of Stockholm makes things a little easier to organise. Add to that the fact that Colin, being the boss, can call time whenever he feels like it, the lads can usually get out of Stockholm in good time on a Friday afternoon. Colin Cotter is also taking his car, saving us money on car rental and giving us plenty of room for baggage. Ciarán O'Reilly will fly down to Copenhagen the next morning and nip back into Sweden by train in time for the throw-in. For the rest of the group I've rented a minibus from the same place.

For those of us with office jobs or more flexible working situations, getting away early is not a problem — even less so for me since I work for myself. But it's not as easy to do a runner from a building site on a Friday afternoon a couple of hours before everyone else without being noticed, so we don't have much chance of getting away too early.

This being the weekend of Princess Viktoria's wedding to her gym instructor boyfriend Daniel, the city is due to close down early for the preparations. I collect the minibus as early as I'm allowed and drive it back to my home on the north side of Stockholm, from where Keith and I will leave later in the afternoon. We aim to get across town and pick up the rest of the lads as quickly as we can, but of course we get stopped in traffic. I wasn't a big fan of royalty to begin with (and you can include the royals of Meath in there too), and I was even less so after sitting waiting for some of them to be allowed to fly past on the motorway. I find it ironic that people who do so little always seem to be in a hurry and I rue the fact that despite chasing a Scandinavian championship this weekend there will be no police escort for us to Malmö. In fact, it's more likely we will be chased by them at some point, especially if Niall Scullion's concrete boot is in control of Colin's accelerator.

We pick up the rest of the lads in the car park at Liljeholmen metro station: big James, Jim, Barry, Seán, Kevin and Niall. There is the usual running around like headless chickens; the metro station has several exits and no one goes to the right one first time out. Just as we are about to leave, the sky is ripped in two by a violent thunderstorm and we all get soaked as we pack the bags into the back of the bus. The rain keeps coming down in a torrential downpour and even with the wipers on it's almost impossible to see anything as we try to find our way back on to the E4 motorway that will lead us to Malmö. I grit my teeth in the driver's seat and my own concrete boot hits the accelerator. I don't mind the long drive, but I aim to make it as short as possible regardless of the damn weather.

There are no girls travelling on this trip, and it is immediately apparent in the level of banter going on in the back of the bus, which has dropped several notches from the previous trip. Gone are the genteel questions about learning foreign languages and the polite drinking games, to be replaced by shouting, roaring and slagging reminiscent of any club back home on the move. Counties are mercilessly hammered for their lack of success on the football or hurling field, with representatives from the likes of Waterford and Roscommon expected to defend their lack of success in the football championship, as if it were even possible. I'm delighted to have another Dub on board for once, especially given that the Dub in question is Seán Beatty. The day he's stuck for a comeback is the day the world will end.

To make the journey as comfortable as possible, we've brought flasks of coffee, water, buns and all manner of snacks and treats. I try not to eat too much junk the day before the game, conscious of the fact that whatever you eat today is going to be your fuel for tomorrow, but sometimes when you're on the road you have no option. Given the choice between stopping for an hour in some restaurant and waiting for the chef to come up with chicken and pasta, I'd rather hit a burger joint and get to our destination as quickly as possible and relax. As the driver of the minibus I have the final say when it comes to the music that gets played, and most of the time the first thing into the CD player is a recording of U2 live from Slane Castle. In the past I've driven the length and breadth of Scandinavia with that CD on and I used to love the bit in the middle of 'Out of Control', where Bono talked about going abroad to get a record deal, but continuing to base their operation in Ireland 'because this is our tribe!' Of course that rings a bit hollow now that they have upped sticks and moved the show out of Ireland because they pay less tax elsewhere.

The age gap is never more apparent than when it comes to selecting what to play on our travels. It's amazing to me that some of the younger lads in the team have never heard the likes of Moving Hearts and Horslips, and other bands that were instrumental in redefining what Irish music was in the seventies and eighties. It seems that Big James from Boston has a better knowledge of ballad singers and their songs than some of the boys born in Ireland, so I sometimes use the minibus as a classroom to introduce them to the likes of the Hothouse Flowers and Planxty. As soon as it gets too much for them I stick on a Frames CD, something which everyone can agree on, and for the first time the level of slagging falls off as the lads sing along.

It's never easy to bend the will of nine different people, regardless of whether it's about what music gets played or when we eat. I plan to only stop once or twice in the 500-odd kilometres, so the choice of cuisine is going to be very limited. Nor am I inclined to stop anywhere that has more than one place to eat; the last thing I want as we make good time towards Malmö is to be spreading ourselves to the four winds at some truck stop in the middle of nowhere.

Besides, the World Cup has been going on in South Africa, so I have a bigger treat up my sleeve for the lads in the back. But I'm saying nothing about that until we stop for something to eat. We drive like the clappers and as the clock ticks on towards eight in the evening we finally pull in to a Burger King for dinner. The doors of the minibus open and its cargo of unruly Gaelic footballers is unloaded on the unsuspecting clientele. There is a massed assault on one of the cash registers as some poor teenage girl from a small country town in the Swedish midlands finds her high school English getting tested like never before. She looks like a rabbit caught in headlights as the myriad of Irish accents is all over her. Big James gets served first; being American, she can actually understand him. The Swedish speakers among us are next, followed by those using a combination of Irish English, pidgin Swedish and violent sign language. Enough food for a small army is ordered and the silent savagery begins, the only noises being the munching of burgers and the crunching of fries, and the occasional shout for 'red sauce' which brings more quizzical looks from the staff.

I finish first and head out to the minibus to fire up the laptop I've brought with me. About six months previously I'd bought a thing called a Slingbox, which basically relays a signal from Ireland over the internet so that I can watch Irish TV wherever I am in the world. You simply connect the TV aerial to one end and a broadband connection in the other, and you can connect to it using a special computer program. I'm not a big TV fan, but it's fantastic to be able to watch sport and news from home live as it happens. There is a debate within the GAA at the present time as to whether games should be provided free to air outside of Ireland as a tool to market the games and generate more interest in them.

One of the most frustrating things I ever encountered was on the day of the All-Ireland hurling final in 2005. With my first child just born I didn't have much time to go to the pub and watch hurling or football on a Sunday afternoon, but thankfully I could listen to the championships on the radio over the internet. The voice of the legendary Micheál Ó Muircheartaigh wafted through our apartment, commentating live from the big game of the week and conveying every ounce of the excitement and the drama that was taking place on the pitch. Even my wife who is no great sports fan got carried away as Micheál swept us along on a wave of colourful language. Even though I had grown up in an era when the coverage of sport was nowhere near as comprehensive as it is today, I was well used to engaging my imagination and allowing the likes of Micheál to paint the pictures for me over the wireless. Back in the studio Micheál's colleagues made sure that no one out in radioland missed a trick, bringing all the latest scores and talking points to their listeners at home and abroad.

Which was all well and good — until the day of the final itself. Galway had dumped perennial favourites Kilkenny out in the semi-final and the stage was set for a titanic struggle against Cork to decide the destination of the title. I made sure to get my family chores done early in the day so that I was free to sit down and enjoy one of the two sporting highlights of the year. I fired up the computer and went on the RTÉ website, ready and waiting for Micheál and the lads to take it one more time from the top and deliver another great show.

At first I thought I'd got the time wrong; having a baby at home is a tiring business and simple mistakes get made, but no, throw-in was only a couple of minutes away. So why then was RTÉ broadcasting a programme about farming? I clicked again and again, different links and different feeds; anything that could be clicked, I clicked on it. But at no point did Micheál's tones fill the kitchen. I was livid. It was too late to rush into town, and besides, an Irish bar on an All-Ireland Sunday is no place for an infant not yet a year old. Instead, I wrote an email to RTÉ, sad, angry and bitter about being robbed of the final.

To their credit RTÉ contacted me the next day. Apparently between themselves and the GAA they hadn't been able to come to an agreement about internet rights for the final, so instead of hearing Seán Óg leading Cork to victory, we were treated to advice on how to manage our chickens. Granted, that's valuable advice especially to Dubs like me, but there's a time and a place for everything. And this was neither the time nor the place.

Living abroad and being chairman of a European club I'm obviously biased, but I can't see why the GAA and the other sporting bodies can't broadcast their games on the internet. I doubt the revenue the GAA gets from European broadcast rights is very much, and whatever it is, it pales into insignificance when compared to the exposure the game would get. I recently went to buy a mobile phone and as I was signing the order form the Swedish sales assistant asked if I was Irish. 'I am,' said I proudly. 'Excellent. Do you know anything about hurling?' came the surprising response. It turned out that he had seen a little report on the All-Ireland hurling final on one of the Eurosport channels and thought it looked very exciting. Ironically, I was in Croke Park for that classic final when Tipperary ended Kilkenny's dominance, and I had brought with me a former Swedish professional footballer, Pelle Blohm, who now works as a journalist and media pundit. The following week his column in a major regional newspaper was given over to the fantastic spectacle he had seen in the home of Gaelic games — proof if ever it was needed of the universal appeal of Gaelic games.

There is also a case to be made for the likes of the soccer team and the rugby team making their games available to viewers living abroad, but this would require a shift in mindset that might only be brought about by legislation, as with the protected list of sporting events in the UK. Over the last number of years virtually every sporting organisation in Ireland has become more and more commercial, with massive deals for TV rights becoming the norm. Naturally the value in TV rights lies in their exclusivity, but given that the lion's share of the TV market is at home on the island of Ireland, surely these games could be made available to Irish people abroad over the internet. The value of such a service to the Irish diaspora cannot be overstated. A love of sport is a defining characteristic in many Irish people, and to deny them the simple opportunity to follow the national teams that represent them is just cruel. Given that many of these organisations are the recipients of large amounts of taxpayers' money, the problem could be easily solved — no internet access for emigrants, no grants. It sounds simplistic and in reality there are other legal issues to be considered, but that's it in a nutshell.

I took the Swedish sales assistant's business card and promised him that the next time we were organising a training session he would be the first name on the list. I just wish I had the mail addresses of everyone else in Sweden who saw that report on Eurosport.

But there is no Gaelic football or hurling at this hour on a

Friday night in June; instead, we will be watching the World Cup
as England are due to meet Algeria. I put in the 3G internet card,
connect everything up and start the viewing program. After a few
seconds, the minibus is filled with the voices of Bill O'Herlihy and
Eamon Dunphy. Word goes around Burger King like wildfire and
for once there's no problem getting the lads back into the bus. No
one wants to see the game more than me, but again I'm the only
one insured to drive the bus, so I won't be able to see it. Because
Seán Beatty is such an excellent soccer player with a good
knowledge of the game as well as having a great sense of humour,
I give him the job of commentating on the game for those of us
sitting in the front.

Bad move. Seán is a great bloke and a wonderful footballer, but
he's no George Hamilton. All sugared up from the visit to Burger
King, his only concern is the fact that he has Gerrard and Rooney
in his World Cup fantasy football team. For 90 minutes no other
player gets a mention as he roars at the two of them in his heavy
Dublin accent, as if they can somehow hear his voice over the
vuvuzelas all the way down in South Africa. He screams at other
players to pass the ball to Rooney, then roundly abuses the
unnamed culprits when they fail to serve up a hat-trick for him
or Gerrard.

'Pass it. Pass it! He's free! Would ya ever pass the fu . . . Ah
Jaysus, he may as well not have bothered. Ah wouldya lookit!
What are ya doin', ya muppet! He's out of my fantasy team now.
Don't know why I put him in it in the first place. He's a bleedin'
donkey.'

By now the rest of the bus is more entertained by Seán than the
brutal football being played by our neighbours across the water,
and the temporary breaks in the internet service only serve to
heighten his frustration. By the time the game ends we are only
half an hour from Malmö and our journey is nearly over. I've only
ever passed Malmö before on the way to Denmark, so it'll be

interesting to see it for the first time. All I have to go on is what I've read in the papers and seen on TV since I moved here, as well as dim and distant memories of the great football team that represented the city back in the late seventies and early eighties. In fact, ABBA and Malmö FF were probably the two main things Irish people of my generation associated with Sweden. Unfortunately the football club couldn't quite match the singing quartet's record in Europe. Whereas ABBA managed to win the Eurovision, Malmö got beaten in the final of the European Cup in 1979 by Brian Clough's Nottingham Forrest.

Since I moved here in 1999, much of the media coverage of Malmö has been about Zlatan Ibrahimovic and the troubled estate of Rosengård that he comes from. Zlatan is an outrageously talented and individualistic soccer player whose style of play is about as far from the traditional Swedish one as you can get, and opinions on him have divided Sweden since he burst on to the scene as a teenager. Some say his emergence marks a development in Swedish culture; that a culture previously based on the collective is now showing signs of embracing the talents of the individual. Others perceive his lack of humility and single-mindedness as arrogance.

The estate from which he comes is often held up as an example of Sweden's failure to properly integrate its immigrant population, and the social problems and high unemployment to be found there give fuel to the fire of those who mistrust other cultures and would like to see the borders closed. In particular, the Muslim population comes in for criticism for their failure to adapt. But integration is about so much more than just moving to a country and finding somewhere to live. Most of the immigrants I have met here, be they from Ireland or Iraq, America or Afghanistan, are delighted to live in such a fantastic and well-organised democracy, and all they want to do is get themselves a job and provide for their families. But sometimes it's not that simple, and until conditions exist whereby people can quickly assimilate, get into the workforce and feel a sense of pride and achievement in what they do every day, the problems will continue. Holding up Zlatan as an example isn't going to help the vast majority of the people who live there.

I'm still undecided about him. I've met him a couple of times when reporting on Sweden's national team for a major news agency and like everyone else in this world he is a complex character, full of all the idiosyncrasies and inconsistencies that mark us out as human beings. He's also a young man who makes his living in a very rarified environment, full of materialism and selfishness. He has the media chasing him to an embarrassing degree and he has to cope with the expectations of people at home and abroad in everything he does. There is no doubt he is one of the best soccer players of his generation, but whether or not he can maximise that potential and win the Champions League remains to be seen. If he doesn't, he can always sign up with Malmö GAA when his career as a professional soccer player is finished; given his physical size and strength and his obvious talent, I hope he waits until long after I've retired from the game. It might be a great marketing coup for Gaelic games, but I for one don't fancy having to mark him.

The city of Malmö itself is in the Skåne region, and the people that inhabit it remind me of the citizens of our own city of Cork back home. To begin with, the locals speak Swedish with an impenetrable accent that almost sounds comical to the ears of those who learned the language anywhere else in the country. They also have a healthy disrespect for the rest of Sweden, much like those from the People's Republic of Cork have for virtually everyone else back home. Over the centuries Skåne was the subject of a massive tug of war between Sweden and Denmark, with both kingdoms enjoying jurisdiction during various different periods of history. The Peace Treaty of Roskilde signed in 1658 actually contained a clause that gave Skåne the right to its own legislature, something the Swedes then nullified in 1720, moving all the administrative functions to Stockholm. Needless to say, this sticks in the craw of the locals and to this day there is a strong nationalist element there who feel that the region should be independent of both Sweden and Denmark.

Almost like a sign of their contrary nature, I'm immediately struck by the conflicting road signs. There seems to be an inner ring road and an outer ring road, and our GPS seems to be unsure which one is the best one to take. As is usual when driving in Europe, missing your exit means driving around for a long time before you get another chance, and eventually we screech across three lanes, footballs and players bouncing around in the back, as I spot the exit for our hostel just a little too late.

We park the minibus and make our way to the reception, passing by the fruit pickers from Eastern Europe and Asia who are here to help out with whatever harvest is up next in Mother Nature's calendar. It's Friday night and many of them are sitting outside smoking and drinking from suspicious-looking bottles of cheap eastern vodka. The atmosphere would be threatening if most of them weren't so obviously blind drunk.

We meet the rest of the lads who have arrived before us. The reception at the hostel is unmanned at this hour of the night, so all our keys and linen are locked into one of the rooms to which we have a code, and Colin is once again working his magic with the rooming list. His organisational skills are second to none, but I'm left wondering how he would have fared if Microsoft had never invented Excel; it seems he has a spreadsheet for everything, from team formations to rooming lists to the amount that everyone owes for their travel and accommodation, right down to the last penny.

Sean's batteries are drained from his commentating as we empty the van of its cargo. As usual I've got a room on my own, but with video cameras and tripods and medical bags I need a hand to get everything up the flight of stairs. The lads duly oblige, dumping the bags outside the door of my single room, and a minute later I'm surveying the narrow bed with a view to getting into it as soon as possible. I let out a heavy sigh, relieved to be finally at our destination. Being the chairman of the club and the driver of the minibus for these trips, I feel a huge sense of responsibility to the lads and girls that travel. And even though they enjoy it every bit as much as I do, I'm deeply grateful to them for their trust in me and the rest of the committee, and that they give so freely of their time and money so that we can all chase this dream together. I lie down on the bed for a minute, knowing there are still a few things to be done. But there's something not quite right, so I wander down the hall to chat to Colin and Niall.

Mark is already dozing off as I enter the lads' room and we're whispering quietly and making small talk, and then it strikes me. The kit. I've left the fucking kit bag behind — in Stockholm, about 400 miles away. All our jerseys and the spare shorts and socks. Fuck!

Now I've been around a long time and been involved in some daft enterprises and situations, so I'm no stranger to that sinking feeling. For the most part it doesn't bother me as long as it's only me that is affected. But that wasn't the case this time. I was the chairman of the club and had taken responsibility for getting everyone and everything we needed down to Malmö in one piece. I'd let the side down. I could stamp and whinge and moan about how I had to hire the bus and drive it and look after everything, but the truth was that I'd taken the responsibility for the kit and I'd forgotten it. End of story. I'd fucked up. Instead of coming down in our classy O'Neills kit to get our revenge for Copenhagen, we were going to end up looking like a bunch of clowns having a kick-about in Fairview Park with a set of smelly old bibs to set us apart from the rest — if we were lucky. After all the hard work we'd put in over the previous weeks and months, I felt well and truly sick and I had no idea what to do to rescue the situation. Whatever credibility we had as a club — and I as chairman of that club — was quickly going down the drain.

We had our red training bibs in one of the kit bags, but as they hadn't been washed for a few weeks they stank to high heaven. With so many games in each tournament, we might be in luck and have time to get to one of the sports stores if they were open. I'd have no hesitation sticking the credit card on the counter to get this problem solved, but then there was the problem of trying to get a full set of shirts numbered at that hour of the morning. What a mess this was turning out to be!

Thankfully Colin Courtney and his legendary organisational skill came to the rescue, with probably the simplest solution of all. Wasn't Ciarán flying down the next morning? Couldn't he collect the kit from my place and bring it with him? I could have cried with relief. Colin came up with a simple straightforward solution to what had previously seemed an impossible problem. Redemption was just a couple of phone calls away, but like everything else it wasn't that straightforward.

Getting Ciarán to collect the kit was no problem. He and I lived in two more or less adjoining suburbs, so all he had to do was hop in his car, bang the address I gave him into the GPS and stop outside my place, where hopefully the kit would be waiting for him. I say hopefully because my missus is not one to stay up late, and she's definitely not one for answering the phone late at night. It was past 11 o'clock and she would have been long in bed by then. The chances of her paying any attention to the phone at that hour of the night were very slim indeed. I rang and rang and, true to form, no one picked up. So near and yet so far.

There was nothing for it but to keep ringing, fearing the worst. I called my neighbour Rami, who had a key to our apartment, but he was in a nightclub somewhere in town and by the sound of things he wasn't planning on going home any time soon. I began thinking about how I would describe our bedroom window to Ciarán so that he could start pegging stones at it to wake her up. Then it struck me that a large Irishman throwing stones at her window around midnight might actually frighten the living daylights out of her and force her even further into hiding. Despair was starting to creep back in again and I was on the verge of giving Ciarán permission to break into our home, when all of a sudden she answered the phone.

'Why do you keep ringing at this hour of the night?' she says, her voice full of exasperation. 'Pick up the damn phone and I'll tell you!' I roar back, before quickly remembering my manners. I need her far more than she needs me right now, and the last thing I need is her banging the phone down, leaving poor Ciarán standing outside with no kit and an early flight fast approaching. I still found it odd that she could lie there whilst the phone rang 20 times in a row and not be in the slightest bit curious as to who it might be. I can only assume that she knew exactly what the problem was and that she simply hoped I would go away.

I describe our predicament to her and she grudgingly agrees to meet Ciarán at the entrance to our apartment building with the heavy O'Neills kit bag. A few minutes later he sends a text to confirm that he has the kit and he'll bring it with him in the morning. I breathe a massive sigh of relief, barely hearing the abuse I'm getting for forgetting the kit. It's embarrassing, but I couldn't care less now that it's solved.

The relief doesn't last long. I head back up to Colin and Niall to tell them the good news, but their news for me is not what I'd hoped for. With so many strong players in the squad, they've decided to drop me from the starting 11 for tomorrow's opening game. It's not unexpected. Most of the other candidates for the forward positions are younger, fitter and faster than me, but it's still a kick in the teeth. I hadn't gone to all this trouble setting the club up just to stand and watch when the games were being played; like any other player, I wanted to be out there in the middle doing my bit.

I had been playing well and scored a couple of decent goals in the sponsors' game a couple of weeks previously, but they explain to me how close it was between me and one of the other lads, and there was very little to choose between us. I knew the squad we travelled down with was probably the strongest we could muster and that there were probably fellas who would be getting less playing time than me, but that was cold comfort when all you want to do is play. Still, there were at least four matches (five if we reached the final) to be played. I had already discussed with Niall about moving out to midfield or half forward for at least some of the games, and I definitely fancied my chances against big Freddie from Oslo as, whatever about his size, he wasn't going to burn me for pace.

After all the excitement of the missing kit, I'm hungry again, so despite the late hour a few of us jump back in the minibus and head into Malmö. The centre of town is packed with Friday night revellers enjoying the summer evening, drinking beer and smoking on the verandas of the pubs and restaurants. We find a late-night shop and stock up on toothpaste, milk and bananas before heading back to the hostel, leaving the partying behind us. Tomorrow night it will be our turn. But first, we have a job to do.

―――

The following morning looks like a perfect day for playing football. We awake to the good news that Ciarán has landed in Copenhagen with the kit, and one of the lads will pick him up from the train station before we head off to the pitch for today's game.

Oddly, given the fact that the lads have dropped me, I was able to relax. The disappointment at being left out is much easier to live with than the prospect of playing from the start, which brings with it all the mental preparation that goes into a game. There were no pre-match nerves to keep me awake, because I wouldn't be starting. As a substitute the expectations are a little bit less. You don't have a defined role to begin with. You end up coming into the game and trying to cover a gap or give another player a rest, so there's no point in even trying to go over the whole thing in your mind. Instead I was able to think about certain specific situations, such as what I'd do if I came on up front, or if Niall wanted me to go in at midfield against Oslo or Copenhagen. I still woke up early and checked the morning papers before heading down for breakfast, but for once I was at ease.

Once again the smokers were out of their beds and down at the door early for the first fag of the day. We soon filled a little section of the breakfast room. Again, the lack of a female presence meant that the level of humour was far short of what it should have been, and it's a blessing that the tourists from Denmark and Germany barely understood a word of the rapid-fire Irish/English hybrid that was being fired around amidst the guffaws of laughter.

As the younger fellas finally made their appearance — with big Declan bringing up the rear as usual — I nipped back up to the room to get another treat for the boys. I came back down with a bag full of Barry's teabags, and the joy and excitement in the breakfast room couldn't have been greater if I had started handing out €50 notes. I promised the boys there would be more teabags for breakfast the following morning — but only if they came home with the trophy that evening.

There was always going to be some stick when Ciarán arrived with the kit, but I wasn't too sensitive about it by this time. It would have been a whole lot worse if it hadn't arrived at all. We went through the familiar ritual of getting half our kit on before heading to the bus and the cars to take us to the ground in good time.

Of those who had travelled, Colin Cotter and Barry Quinn were both suffering injuries and wouldn't be able to play, but that still left us with too many players for the day. I wasn't the only one who was going to be disappointed.

The pitch for the day was right beside the sea, with only a big dune protecting us from the breeze. We were wary of the sun getting up as it had in Denmark, and having been burned to a cinder there, we were better prepared this time around. Before the jerseys were handed out, various factors of sun cream were passed around first.

This was the first time I'd seen any of the Malmö lads since their acceptance speech down in Copenhagen. They were all nice fellas but for some reason a few things from that tournament still irked me: Brian wearing the pink shorts, the huddle with the big shout at the end, and the fact that they didn't give us a mention in their victory speech. I'm sure none of this was meant, but judging by some of the friendly slagging that was going on via Facebook and some of the comments that were being made, I wasn't so sure. There was no doubt their plan had worked in the final in Copenhagen, but I wasn't so sure lightning would strike twice for them — especially not now with extra players in our squad.

The addition of Ciarán meant we had to rearrange the seating plans to make sure everyone got to the pitch at the same time. From the hostel it was more or less a straight run down past the magnificent Swedbank stadium to the seafront and Limhamnfältet, which would be our base for the day.

When we arrived at the road which should have led us to the seafront, we came to a T-junction. Give any Irishman the choice of two ways to go, and nine times out of ten he'll choose the wrong one; and I did. We drove along the seafront looking for somewhere to swing off so that we could get back to where we had seen the Gaelic football goals set up for the tournament. A sharp swing into a car park got us facing in the right direction but still left us a drive across untouched grass if we were to get to the pitch. As we drove slowly over the well-cut grass an Indian-looking man came running out, shouting and waving. It was then that we discovered we were driving across the cricket pitch he was marking out for a match there on the same day. Already halfway across his pitch, there was nothing for it but to keep going. Needless to say, when we finally arrived at the Gaelic football pitch, they told us we should have taken a left instead of a right at the T-junction. Not only would we have got there quicker; we could have avoided the embarrassing international sporting incident with our cricket-playing friends from the subcontinent.

The pitch in Malmö was an improvement on the one in Copenhagen, much flatter and with proper goals constructed from scaffolding poles. The rugby goals we had used in Copenhagen were a bit off-putting as they had two crossbars. If the ball hit the upper (rugby) one, it counted as a point as under normal circumstances the ball would have flown over the bar.

On the field beside us one of the local Australian Rules clubs is setting itself up for the day, and a barbecue and a bar are being built. Australian Rules seems to be very popular in Scandinavia with clubs dotted all over Sweden and Denmark, and rumour has it that these two countries are two of the strongest in the sport outside the mother country itself. The Aussies turn their games into events, with families invited along to take part and enjoy the day out. There was no sense in both the Aussies and Malmö GAA setting up bars, so today we'll be making some use of their hospitality.

Our team is scattered around in all directions. Niall wants

them back in one place to give out the shirts and get on with a bit of a warm-up and kick the ball around a little. I'm laying the shirts out on the ground with Colin when it hits me again that I won't be getting one. I hadn't thought of the fact that this particular part of the day happens in public. Will the rest of the lads be looking at me to see what my reaction will be? Will they even be bothered? I decide I'm not going to say or do anything either way. What is important today is not whether I play or not. What is important is that we win this tournament in Malmö's backyard. My chance will come again I've no doubt.

Big James is understandably disappointed not to make it into the 15 that will make up the match squad to begin with. Despite the fantastic improvements he has made in his game, Niall and Colin can't afford to be sentimental, and when it comes to cutting the squad from 16 to 15, James winds up on the wrong side of the line. As it turns out, he will get more game time than some of the Stockholm players today, as Gothenburg can't believe their luck to find such a big, strong player available. Even though this will mean he will gain a vast amount of championship football experience, he's not happy and understandably so. He came down to Malmö with the same aim as the rest of us: to win the tournament with his club, not to make up the numbers.

For me the bad news isn't finished yet, and Scullion calls the lads together for a warm-up. As mentioned before, my innate laziness when it comes to training and the fact that I'm dubious about the value of intensive warm-ups means I'm not first in the queue when this one is starting. My nose is already slightly out of joint due to being dropped, so this runaround is a serious test of my patience. This is neither the time nor the place for a discussion about the merits or otherwise of warm-ups, but as there is a wait of over an hour before our first game is due to start, I see little point in expending energy now that we might well need later on in the day. As a silent and admittedly cowardly protest I started filling water bottles and generally tried to avoid taking part as much as I could.

Colin comes back with the news that the schedule is pretty similar to what it was in Copenhagen, which means the other teams will all play each other before we make our entrance into the fray. Essentially, our plan is to do exactly what we did in Copenhagen but make it last a little longer.

The atmosphere in our team today is markedly different from the first tournament. For one thing, we're not the new boys any more. We know exactly what to expect from each of these teams, and even if Malmö are slight favourites for the tournament, we know we can take them. The additions to our squad have made us a lot stronger and have given us far more options than we had in Copenhagen. Regardless of who is in the 15-man squad for each game, we will have four strong players on the bench who can come in and do a job, so there is no need for our starting 11 to run themselves into the ground.

And even though the banter and friendship and camaraderie is still there, there's a different tone to it. Today is about winning, and there is no time for sympathy or empathy or anything else. As usual we applauded the lads as their names were called out and they were handed their jersey for the day, but when it came to Colin handing me the number 12, or James being handed the 'number 16', there was no 'hard luck lads, you'll get your chance'. This was it. We had a tournament to win, and everyone had their part to play. Accept it, get on with it, and if you get the chance, prove the coaches wrong. But if you plan to go around moping, you may as well just sit in the bus and wait for the ride home.

In another positive development, there's a different referee for this tournament, and as I thought John Kelleher was a little bit slow to blow the whistle in Copenhagen, this might not be a bad thing. It turns out that the new ref, Shay O'Doherty of Maastricht GAA club, is an old friend of the Sundbyberg Express. When Karl introduces me to Shay, I waste no time telling him to watch out for the rough stuff from Malmö, and anyone else for that matter. Even though our squad for this tournament is physically much stronger, I don't want anyone thinking they can take liberties with us. Shay seems to be a decent enough lad and shows himself to be a very competent, fair and level-headed referee throughout the day.

Shay moves off to get the proceedings under way, and once again it will be Malmö facing off against Copenhagen to start the day. We are the non-playing club assigned to umpiring duties, and I make it my business to volunteer as one of the four. I want the lads to see that I'm prepared to do whatever is needed to make my contribution to our success. If I was playing I wouldn't have a whole lot of interest in standing around by the goal. I'd much prefer to be sitting somewhere in the shade and conserving my energy, but instead I'll be an umpire and let Ciarán and the rest of the lads have a rest. It gives me a closer look at the goalkeepers I might soon be testing, and I can't say I was sorry to miss part of the warm-up Niall was putting the lads through behind the goal.

Tactically, there would be a few subtle differences this time out. No stone had been left unturned since the Copenhagen game, and the videos were watched and analysed to find out where we came up short. Phil Cahill was consulted and long discussions were had as to what could be improved with the players we had at our disposal. With Colin's speed and Ciarán's power up front, Niall wanted to hit them early if at all possible and put our opponents on the back foot. If that wasn't on, we were to stick to our usual short-passing game. To give us plenty of options to do this around the midfield, the half forwards were to pull out a little bit more, which would give the two lads up front more space to run into.

In the previous tournament a single point separated Malmö

from Copenhagen in the first game, but this time out it was a different story. Malmö started strongly while Copenhagen never seemed to get out of the blocks, and Jakob Bak Simonsen in the Danish goal found himself under attack from the very first minute. With Copenhagen and Malmö only separated by a narrow stretch of water, the Danes were the visiting team that had the shortest journey to the tournament, and from my position as umpire they seemed to have a pretty strong team, but they never seemed to click at all. An unpredictable breeze coming in from the sea wasn't helping matters either, and it seemed to snatch Jakob's kick-outs and dump them where Copenhagen's players least expected them. A couple of quick goals either side of half-time put paid to the Danish challenge, and Malmö ran out easy winners, this time by ten points.

Oslo were up next against Gothenburg, and the Norwegian lads had clearly been putting in time and effort on the training field as they proved a much harder nut for Billy and the boys to crack this time out. With big Freddie storming about the place as usual, the Norwegians managed to keep possession much better, and indeed they even managed to net their first goal in competitive football when Freddie smashed one home to take the lead. With the Oslo players swarming all over them, Gothenburg had struggled offensively. The Norwegians displayed great discipline at the back, and the mercurial Adrian Kelly was denied his usual haul of frees that regularly puts him among the top scorers in any tournament. But it's hard to keep a skilful player like Adrian down, and he popped up to score a crucial goal in the second half and put Gothenburg back in the driving seat. Stalwart Billy Finn secured the win with a storming run from the back before popping over a point to round things off. Tournament play is like a chess match, with the need to win the current game balanced by the need to conserve energy for future challenges throughout the day. Even though they got a scare, Gothenburg were delighted to get out of there with a win. Then it was our turn.

Niall was putting the boys though their second warm-up and, frankly, the results were alarming. Instead of running through some smooth drills at high speed and frightening the life out of any opponent who might be watching, the balls were spraying all over the place as mishit passes bounced and bobbled past their intended targets. Maybe it was nerves. Maybe things would be better as soon as we settled down and got stuck into the game properly.

As the warm-up ended and Niall and Colin imparted the last few words of advice, I put my tracksuit top back on and headed back towards the line where Barry was looking after our big TV camera. I know Barry was probably very disappointed with the lack of playing time he got in Copenhagen and I was pleased for his sake that this time at least he had a reason not to be playing. With his injured fingers strapped together, he could barely hold a ball let alone catch one or tackle someone. But I was feeling fully fit and better than I had done in many years, and here I was standing on the sideline. I got the same helpless feeling as I had towards the end of the final in Copenhagen, when the rest of the team struggled manfully but couldn't get the ball up to the forward line. A bundle of nervous energy, I would have to control myself until my chance came. In particular, I had to keep my trap shut; nervous energy often gets translated into abuse of the referee, and the last thing I wanted to do was antagonise Shay. He had done a great job in difficult circumstances in the first game, and his level of refereeing was just about perfect in my opinion.

Shay called the two team captains over to point out what he would be coming down hard on in the game and to toss the coin. In the meantime I had a quick chat with Ciarán to let him know what to expect from his first tournament. Playing against these players in these short games required a different approach. For one thing, it was very easy to get frustrated up front when you're not seeing too much of the ball, but you have to resist the temptation to drift out too much; otherwise you'll end up crowding out your half forwards and midfielders, and when you do get on the ball, you'll be too far away from the danger area to do any damage. I told him he needed to be selfish: if he got the ball, turn and head for goal, and if they took him down he'd get a free or a penalty, and if not he'd have an easy score. Ciarán is a very clever chap and I could see him taking all this in, but I'm not sure he believed me when I told him how hard it was sometimes to get on the ball. He'd soon find out.

From the first throw-in against Malmö it was obvious that we'd stepped up a gear. John Carroll looked like he was born to play in the centre of a Gaelic football pitch, and his ability to get on the ball anywhere on the park and make space for himself was an absolute godsend to his team mates. Sean Beatty was doing what Sean Beatty does best, annoying people, covering the ground and getting through an enormous amount of work. Not even Kevin Moran, who went on to play professionally for Manchester United, looked as much like a soccer player playing Gaelic football as Sean Beatty did. He was superb, and whatever about the rest of us running out of steam, there was little chance he would. If he did, all we'd have to do was give him a couple of desserts from Burger King and he'd be back to himself in no time.

Kevin Carroll was also back to his best and showing no sign of the hamstring injury that had caused his premature exit from the Copenhagen tournament. What Kevin gives a half forward or half back line is not just tremendous ability on the ball; he's also a tenacious and aggressive defender who doesn't believe there's any such thing as a lost cause. Kevin will chase you and chase you until you simply give up; then he'll take the ball off you and go up the other end and score. That said, it's very hard to play that style of football and come back after an injury. Hamstrings and groins are notoriously sensitive and in rushing back into a game — especially high-speed, competitive games like this one — there's always a risk that it will go again. I was keeping warm on the sideline just in case.

Having seen the way we were playing I had no doubt we were going to win this game, and there is nothing easier than stepping into a winning team. True, Malmö were able to pop over a quick point at the beginning of the game, but by this stage we were so used to losing the throw-in that someone scoring from it didn't bother us. It was like a 'gimme'. We'd let them have that one at the start of each half, but everything else, they'd have to work for.

It didn't take long for John Carroll's class to show. He started in midfield but gave himself the freedom to turn up wherever he needed to be on the pitch, always providing an outlet for a pass and directing play as he went. Malmö were barely able to get their hands on the ball at all, and when John fired home our first goal of the day after only a few minutes, there was never likely to be any way back for them.

When Malmö did get hold of the ball, they had to contend with a resurgent Kevin Carroll. The team captain looked like he had brought with him all the pent-up energy from the tournament in Copenhagen, and was flying from the first whistle. Kevin's play is not just about tenacity and energy; he is a very skilful footballer, a sweet striker of the ball with great technique, and when a breaking ball was won around the centre of the pitch, it was to him or John Carroll that the Gaels looked to move the ball up the pitch.

But when an injury did come, it was to Ciarán. From the beginning I could see he was having a bit of difficulty getting to grips with the game and Ginge wasn't making it any easier for him. Whenever the ball did get played in to him, he had little or no time to do anything with it before the big hits started flying in.

Kerry-born scoring machine Colin Courtney, a brilliant footballer and co-founder of the Gaels. (*Courtesy of Colin Cotter*)

Gothenburg's Niall O'Connor stretches as he prepares to face Seán Beatty (9) and Colin Courtney (*far right*) in Malmö. Captain Kevin Carroll is on the far left. (*Courtesy of Colin Cotter*)

Niall Scullion (4) arrives in support as Courtney makes a break for it. (*Courtesy of Colin Cotter*)

The author takes a quick free kick as Billy Finn and John Carroll look on. (*Courtesy of Colin Cotter*)

Niall Scullion launches another stylish effort at the posts. Though aiming for a point, this one would drop sharply over the keeper's head for a goal. (*Courtesy of Colin Cotter*)

One team trying to catch him, the other trying to get out of his way, Colin Courtney accelerates towards goal. (*Courtesy of Colin Cotter*)

Referee Shay O'Doherty shows our ever-committed captain Kevin Carroll a yellow card for a clothesline tackle. (*Courtesy of Colin Cotter*)

A grim-faced Oslo goalkeeper heads to his position for the second half. (*Courtesy of Colin Cotter*)

Niall Scullion doing what he does best, breaking at speed out of our half back line to set up another attack. (*Courtesy of Colin Cotter*)

Colin Courtney and his marker enjoying the view of the Malmö 'Turning Tower' during a break in play.

Colin Courtney (*far left*) watches anxiously with the rest to see if his shot hit the back of the net. It did. (*Courtesy of Colin Cotter*)

The author reads the Oslo kick-out, well aware that Freddie is lurking. (*Courtesy of Colin Cotter*)

James Guanci (*left*) gets some tips from Niall Scullion (4) and Ken Feely (8) as Ciarán O'Reilly (*far right*) watches the action. (*Courtesy of Colin Cotter*)

The soft-spoken Niall Scullion (obscured by number 8 Ken Feely) holding a team talk before the final against Malmö. (*Courtesy of Colin Cotter*)

Malmö plot to defend their title on home turf. (*Courtesy of Colin Cotter*)

The peerless Brian Boyd of Malmö wrong-foots the Gaels defence. (*Courtesy of Colin Cotter*)

Probably the fittest man on our—or any—team, Karl 'The Sundbyberg Express' Lambert, makes a break against Malmö. (*Courtesy of Colin Cotter*)

A gracious Malmö side congratulate the Gaels, who have just beaten them in their own backyard to win the tournament. (*Courtesy of Colin Cotter*)

Exhausted but delighted, the Gaels warm down after their first tournament victory. (*Courtesy of Colin Cotter*)

The author holds the Malmö trophy aloft on the morning after the tournament victory. *Left to right*: Niall Balfe, Liam Ginnane, Barry Quinn, John Carroll, the author, Karl Lambert, Keith Hearne, Jim Kelly, James Guanci. (*Courtesy of Colin Cotter*)

Barry Quinn (*right*) presents Liam Ginnane with the poc fada trophy 'liberated' from Billy Finn. Our Liam only got one puck to Billy's two and was declared the winner by his team mates. (*Courtesy of Colin Cotter*)

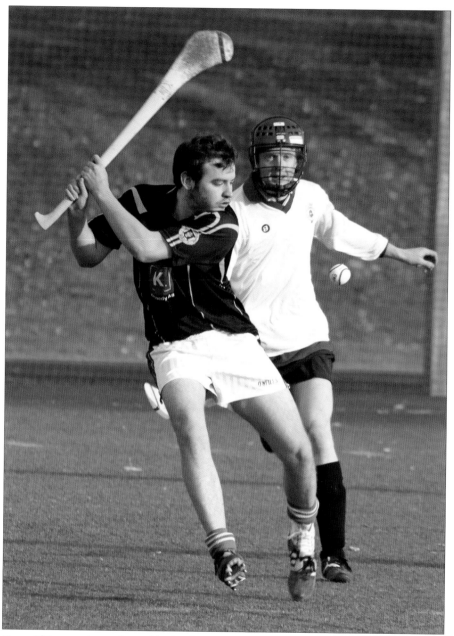

Barry O'Connor shoots for goal in October 2010 as hurling returned to Stockholm after a 15-year absence. (*Author photo*)

Declan Graham lines up a penalty in the Ambassador Cup seven-a-side tournament final, October 2010. (*Author photo*)

The John Aherne trophy on display at the Irish Embassy in Stockholm.

Nigel O'Reilly speeds away from Peter Conroy in the final of the club's seven-a-side tournament, the Ambassador Cup. (*Author photo*)

Bostonian James Guanci proudly displays some of the medals and trophies collected in his first-ever season as a Gaelic footballer, October 2010. (*Author photo*)

The Stockholm Gaels parade their trophies on the steps of Stockholm's Concert Hall, October 2010. (*Courtesy of Éanna and Niamh Kennedy*)

But he's not the kind of guy that hides in a game, and he continued demanding the ball. The next time he got it he was clobbered with a bang on the head, and with blood running from his mouth the referee had no choice but to ask him to leave the field. As he did, the call came for me to take his place. My chance had come a lot earlier than I expected and I was ready to go, but it's very hard to be pleased for yourself when one of your friends has just been hurt.

As I replaced Ciarán, there was almost a tinge of regret. It was actually hugely enjoyable to watch these guys play football from the sideline and marvel at the brilliant players we had in the club. Take Colin Courtney. He would come tearing out from full forward to get on the ball, turning sharply, often dumping his marker on his backside as soon as he got it. Defenders had worked out reasonably quickly that he favoured his left foot and tried to force him on to his right. That didn't bother him one bit. I have never seen a player solo the ball or hit it with such conviction with what coaches would call his 'weaker' foot as Colin Courtney does. As he lofted a point from a tight angle with his right boot, it became apparent that the coaches would have to come up with a new term, because Courtney doesn't have a 'weaker' foot.

With all these fantastic players clicking and playing at the top of their game, it was hard not to get carried away, and for the first time I felt I could play freely and not worry about making a mistake. However badly I might screw up, the team we had on the field was more than capable of making up for it, and as long as they didn't all get hit by a bus, there was little chance of any of the other teams there on the day giving us a hiding. I got stuck in from the very beginning, running around shouting for the ball but not actually seeing a whole lot of it.

The scoring system in Gaelic football makes it a bit of an odd fish in team sports. In most other sports the general idea is to get the ball to the man in the best position to score and let him have a crack. In basketball the ball will be passed around until it gets into the hands of a guy who has an open shot or a run at the basket, whilst in rugby the runner is always looking for the man on the overlap to cross the line and score a try. But in Gaelic football the waters are a little bit muddier. Points can be scored from quite some distance out, and unless you score from within a couple of yards there is always at least one other player who is also in a threatening position and would have a good chance of making a score. Then there are players like Niall Scullion or Adrian Kelly of Gothenburg; give these guys an open look at the posts and they'll pop the ball over nine times out of ten no matter where they are on the field.

Then there is the choice all teams face when attacking: should we go for a goal or a point? The closer you get to the goal the more crowded things tend to get, the more defenders you encounter and the more likely they are to clobber you to stop you from scoring. So on the surface it makes more sense to keep picking off points from a safe distance and build up a lead. But with a goal being worth three points in Gaelic football, that lead can be quickly wiped out — something all the more apparent when our group games are only 20 minutes long. Other than John Carroll's wise mantra, 'take your points and the goals will come', we don't have a scoring strategy as such. We just hope the players on the ball are smart enough to make the right decisions and do what is best for the team.

Every forward likes to make his contribution on the scoreboard, and conscious of the fact that Ciarán might stop the bleeding and declare himself fit at any point, I decided if I did get a chance I was going to do my best to make it count. I didn't have long to wait, and just before half-time it came.

For all the possession we had, we weren't doing enough damage. We should have been well out of sight by half-time, but it felt like we were trying to walk the ball into the net on occasion, and as a result we were passing up easy scores that would quickly have opened up an insurmountable gap. For some silly reason I found myself thinking of Johan Cruyff and the famous Dutch football team in the 1974 World Cup final. Cruyff and the boys came out and basically walked the ball into the West German net from the tip-off. Though they played brilliantly for the following 90 minutes, they still got beaten 2-1. Despite being mauled in the first half, Malmö were just the kind of side that could regroup and punish us if we didn't put them away. So it was time to start putting some daylight between the two teams.

Mark O'Kane collected the ball deep in our half, and after a quick exchange of hand passes he was away up the pitch like a flash. I peeled off to the right to give him an option and shouted for the ball. It was asking a lot of Mark's ability to reach me with the ball and I didn't think for a second he'd even try it. But true to form, he hit it perfectly into my path. Unfortunately I slowed up and let in my old nemesis Ginge in front of me to poke the ball away. I was livid. I was beaten to the first ball that came my way. But there was no time for recrimination as Kevin picked up the rebound. Kevin darted infield, running into traffic as he tried to pass the ball. I broke off his shoulder to his right and he squeezed a perfect ball through a tight gap to leave me free with just the goalkeeper to beat.

The situation was a mirror image of the one in the very first game back in Copenhagen a month previously, and I was determined that the outcome would be the same. Ciarán had played well until he got that smack in the mouth and in truth he was the better player, but I was determined to show Colin and Niall that leaving me on the bench was a decision not to be taken lightly as I took a bounce and flashed a shot past the keeper and into the back of the net. You could hear the wind go out of some of the Malmö players as the ball was picked out of the goal. They had defended tigerishly, but even when they won the ball another wave of black shirts was waiting to attack them again. The subsequent kick-out rose in the air as Shay blew for half-time. One touch, one goal. Not a bad first half off the bench, I thought, as Niall Balfe ran on with the water bottles. Not bad at all.

The half-time team talk didn't consist of much, and it didn't have to. Our tails were up, the confidence levels high, and the football we were playing was brilliant at times. It was odd to see the Malmö players so bereft of ideas. Playing us at home after the physical and psychological beating they had inflicted on us in the final in Copenhagen, we expected them to come out fighting, and we were prepared for another war of attrition. But shorn of the physical side of their game by the referee, there didn't seem to be a plan B. Consigned to chasing shadows for much of the first half, they tired midway through, and even when chances did present themselves, they didn't seem to have the energy to take them. Brian Boyd, imperious in Copenhagen despite the pink shorts, made a break from midfield only to drop the ball straight into our goalkeeper's arms. Under normal circumstances Brian would hit balls like that over the bar in his sleep, but in this game nothing was going right for his team. At the other end Colin Courtney popped over a point for us, and from the resulting kick-out the ball went straight to John Carroll, who gratefully accepted the gift and popped over another.

The second half didn't get any better for our biggest rivals, and even playing at a slightly lower tempo we still ran out comfortable winners by nine points. We had put down a marker against the home side. This tournament was ours for the taking.

It might have been early days, but we were delighted with ourselves following that victory. We had played entertaining football at breakneck speed and soaked up the physical challenge that Malmö had offered. Our nine scores had come from all over the field, but the risk of Cruyff-like complacency hung over us. Having played inter-county football for Antrim, no one knew better than Niall that there are no victories handed out in championship football; they have to be earned. He quickly silenced the euphoria of the victory. No one was handing out any prizes yet and if we wanted to walk away with the trophy, we would need to repeat that performance four more times.

Gothenburg were up next, and even though Ciarán's wound had long since stopped bleeding, my goal against Malmö seemed to have done enough to guarantee me a starting place in the line-up. I was to start on the left side of the half forward line marking Eoin O'Broin, the strong, wiry Dubliner who had travelled down to the first tournament in our minibus. I wasn't the only one in a new position as Niall shuffled our pack considerably. Colin joined Seán Beatty at midfield as Declan moved into the forward line. I felt sorry for big James who lined out in midfield for the opposition; he would be facing two of the best players we had.

We began where we left off, Ken Feely slotting over a point almost from the throw-in. Gothenburg replied with a magnificent point from Adrian, only for Niall to work a fortuitous goal. Again the attack started as Mark broke from the back, and as Niall shaped to shoot from distance, it looked like we would be chalking up another point. But the ball dipped viciously in the breeze over the keeper's head and into the net for a goal. Gothenburg weren't to be outdone and clawed their way back into the game when Liam Ginnane could only parry a speculative punt of theirs into our net.

We weren't too worried. With Colin, Seán and John mopping up in midfield, we had plenty of chances and we were moving the ball well. Niall found me close to goal and called for the return, but instead of giving it back I took a shot, straight into the outstretched arms of Billy Finn. Niall roared his disapproval and I instantly thought, that's gonna cost me later. If you're going to have a shot blocked in front of the posts, try not to do it when the coach is wide open and screaming for the ball back. I barely took a look at the posts for the rest of the first half and instead concentrated on passing the ball for others to take easy scores. As the half drew to a close I found Colin out to my left. Aware that he was one of our danger men, the defence collapsed on top of him, leaving me completely free in the middle. But I barely bothered to call for the ball back, instead leaving him in peace to hammer it home. Half-time came, and sure enough the bench beckoned for me.

The start of the second half was a scrappy affair. The changes we made led to confusion as to who should mark whom and Gothenburg had an unnecessarily easy ride until John Carroll dinked home another lovely goal for us. The economy of effort was superb: having fooled the keeper into going one way, all he had to do was roll the ball over the line and into the net.

Ken Feely was another one putting in a Trojan effort. Niall and Colin subsequently told me it had been between Ken and me for the eleventh and final place in the starting line-up against Malmö, with Ken getting the nod. His style of play is unorthodox and very quick. He plays the game at such a pace that most of the time he looks like the seat of his pants is on fire. Ken could be flying down the wing in one direction when, realising he's about to run out of space, he stops abruptly and heads off in the other direction, all at a hundred miles and hour. That he manages to hang on to the ball in such situations is nothing short of miraculous. But he does, and he gets some spectacular solo scores as a result.

The second goal proves too much for Gothenburg and there is no way back for them. In a way I feel sorry for them. The city has nowhere near the numbers of Irish that we have available to us in Stockholm, and Billy and the lads have a constant struggle to attract and keep players. Yet they are one of the most consistent sides in the championship. Moulded in Billy's image, they are tough and skilful, never giving up without a fight. Englishman Phil Sprackers in the Gothenburg goal has been a revelation since they discovered him. A tremendous shot-stopper with an accurate kick-out, he would slot into any team in Europe. Today they have also added big James to their ranks, without whom they would only have had ten players to take the field. They battle hard, but given the lack of substitutes it's no surprise when they wilt towards the end of the second half, and we can chalk up our second victory of the day, again by a nine-point margin.

For my own part, it's going pretty well. The confidence gained by netting the goal against Malmö is still going strong despite the block by Billy when I should have passed to Niall. I got a second run late in the second half against Gothenburg, and sure enough an opportunity to redeem myself appeared. But out of nowhere Billy appeared once again to block my goal-bound shot. I was incredulous, as I had no idea where he had come from, but in fairness it was typical of Billy's supernatural ability to get himself into the right place at the right time to thwart my efforts.

It was getting harder and harder for Niall to keep the team talks realistic. Gothenburg had given it a right go, but in the end our players and the smart use of our bench helped us on the road to victory. If we kept going like this, it threatened to be a walk in the park. But the job still wasn't done, and there were never any medals handed out before lunchtime. Niall rightly reminded us of what had happened in Copenhagen, when we won our first three games with relative ease, only to struggle badly in the last two. Even with our strong players and the depth of the bench we had available to us, we would still need to keep the tempo up and keep making the right decisions to keep the streak going. Malmö had bounced back from their defeat by us and looked much more dangerous when sticking four goals past Oslo. The schizophrenic Copenhagen side seemed to have finally woken up against the Norwegians, knocking 4-7 past them and not conceding a single score.

Caution was the keyword when taking on Oslo. To date they

had been the whipping boys, but we took nothing for granted, and it's a measure of how seriously we took the game that we started with Declan and John. To progress to the final we needed a result and an early break forward from half back Niall Scullion almost ended the game before it even began. But his shot cannoned back off the crossbar. Kevin Carroll fired over a point shortly afterwards to steady the nerves, but for the most part easy chances went awry as a wasteful Stockholm side struggled with its shooting.

John Carroll steadied the ship with a point before Mark made one of his patented breaks. A flurry of hand passes followed before the ball wound up in the hands of Courtney, who rolled it in for a goal. But the nerves weren't settled yet, and not a minute later the Kerry man shot straight into the goalkeeper's legs when it would have been easier to score. A goal and a point late in the half from John Carroll rescued the situation, and we could breathe easy. Hold this lead and we were in our second consecutive final.

Niall's accountant brain was doing overtime totting up the scores and the permutations when the penny dropped. 'Can you do it?' he asked me. 'Can you go in and do a job on the big man?' 'Damn right,' I said.

Freddie had been quiet during the first half, not getting on the ball and not doing too much damage, and that was exactly the way Niall wanted to keep it. At this stage we were already there, and if we could give the likes of Declan and John Carroll a break now, they'd have plenty left in the tank for the final.

The game passed us by to begin with. I made one break up the middle, only to bobble the ball and lose it to Freddie as I headed for goal. The next time he got it, it was my turn to try and pop it loose from the grip of the giant. Seán Beatty then chased down a lost cause to keep the ball in play and made a lovely pass to me inside the square with Freddie behind me. As I caught the ball and went to turn, the haymakers rained in from left and right. It was like being hit by a car and by the time the fourth punch hit me in the back, it was obvious to all concerned that Freddie was making no effort to play the ball — everyone except the referee, of course, who waved play on.

I was fuming. The primary job of the referee in any sport is to protect the players, and it was getting to the point where we all needed protection from Freddie. Twice more in the game he put in dangerous challenges on me, one in the area, which was waved off, before I was finally given a free kick for being hit after the ball was long gone. I was so annoyed with Shay that I missed the point from an embarrassingly short distance. Shay told me later that night that he agreed with me and that the first incident in particular should have been a penalty, but like John Kelleher in Copenhagen, he thought we were already miles ahead and that sending Freddie off and awarding us a penalty would only ruin the game for all concerned. It was a decision that was to have far-reaching consequences in the next tournament.

Taking a break at full forward, Declan Graham atones for my miss by slotting home a third goal and the job is done. The final is just around the corner, but first there's the small matter of an unbeaten record to defend.

The Copenhagen game is academic in one way as we're already through, but none of us seems to have a grasp of what effect it would have on the rest of the teams should we lose. Even though we need to rest players for the final, there's still no doubt that we are going into this game to win it. No matter what way you reshuffle this particular pack, in the end it's going to be a pretty strong team out on the pitch.

Having kept Freddie relatively quiet and taken whatever he had to throw at me, Niall has decided to give me a chance in an all-Dublin midfield beside Seán Beatty against Copenhagen. My job will be to keep things ticking over, play smart and not let them come rushing through us. I'm not expecting to start the final, and with the lads so caught up in their own game, there's a risk that this might be the last chance I have to make a contribution, so I'm going to grab it with both hands.

Beatty and I line up for the throw-in and I find myself paired against Copenhagen's Seán Coogan. Seán is about half my age and twice as fast. When he saw me line up alongside him he must have thought all his Christmasses had come together. Beatty runs off to mark Simon, only to be stopped in his tracks by a shout from me.

'Where the fuck do you think you're goin?'

'I'm marking me man!'

'That's my man, sunshine. Your man is right here. But he won't be for long.'

Any other player would probably have argued, but not Seán. Chasing young Coogan around for the next 20 minutes or so will be a pleasure for Cabra's finest.

Simon and I are well matched, even if he does have a burst of acceleration that is scary at times. I have the beating of him in the air, and if I can just manage to keep him on the back foot he hopefully won't have the room to use his pace to burst past me. As long as I don't dive in to any mad tackles I should be OK.

Playing midfield is like a game of chess with hundreds of small decisions that can affect the outcome of the game. I'm content to let Simon wander a little bit and occasionally pick up the ball in his half back line. It's not that he can't use the ball well (his left foot is razor sharp and could land the ball on a postage stamp), but I have confidence in the guys behind me to mop up any quick balls he tries to play in there.

Meanwhile I'm doing my best to make myself available. With the other lads trying to save their legs for the final, it's up to the likes of Niall, Keith and me to do the lion's share of the running in this game, with the starters playing about half a game each. All the movement gets me into some good positions and I finish the first half with a nice point.

The second half sees wholesale changes, with the reserves brought on to do the donkey work. Beatty makes way for John Carroll as Mark O'Kane drops into goal leaving Liam Ginnane to come out the field. Colin pops up at corner forward and Niall strolls through the second half as only a class player like him can, conserving energy but still making a telling contribution.

I'm growing into the midfield role as we get more comfortable. Simon gets away from me early in the half and pops over a great point from way out on the left touchline, but other than that he's not getting away from me too easily. I push up behind our half forwards in an effort to be the extra man and fashion a goal chance, but there's nothing doing. I drop back a little and pick up the ball from Niall, and all of a sudden I spy an opening for a shot at the posts. Having been burned twice by Billy's blocks, I'm loath to let fly, but if you don't shoot you can't score, and we need to get some points on the board. The ball arcs nicely, bouncing off the crossbar and over for a point. I would have been happy with that when I hit it; now I'm regretting that it didn't dip under the bar for a goal.

We start to pull away from them now. A couple of frees from Colin puts a bit of daylight between the two sides. Niall plays me in again and I drop the shoulder to go round a defender before slotting over another one. I'm starting to really enjoy this now. It's a long time since I've been on the ball this much, and I can see why Ciarán was getting frustrated up front, where he was seeing the ball about as often as Haley's comet in some games.

Another run and I almost put Keith in for a goal before Shay blows the final whistle. I've done a lot of running and my legs feel heavy, but having collected three of our eight points and only conceded two as a team, I'm as happy as I've been all day. The result may not have had any bearing on the standings from our point of view, but winning is never a bad habit, and those of us who started the day on the bench certainly didn't want to be given a chance to play, only to blow it by losing the game. James had been called back into our squad too; having played for Gothenburg all day, we needed him now to make a contribution to keeping Copenhagen quiet. The big Bostonian went in at full forward; with a little more luck he would have marked his championship debut in the black jersey with a goal.

What awaits us now is a short break for a puc fada competition, where each contestant tries to hit a hurling ball (sliotar) as far as possible. Then comes the match we've been waiting a month for — a reprise of the Copenhagen final against Malmö in their own backyard. At stake is a tournament victory and the chance to stake a claim in the race for the Scandinavian title — and for us, a shot at revenge.

For all our victories so far on the day and the fancy passing and the clinical finishing, Malmö are still in the driving seat. Points are awarded for your place in the tournament, with the winner of each tournament final getting 25 points, the loser getting 20 and so on down. Before the throw-in Malmö are still at the top of the table and a win here will stretch their lead in the Scandinavian championship to ten points with two tournaments to go. This would mean we would have to win the last two tournaments and hope they slipped up somewhere along the line and didn't make a final. Our victory over them early in the day means nothing if we don't beat them and close the gap in the standings.

Despite the fact that they relish a bit of rough stuff, Malmö are a very good footballing team, and in Dave Fahy they have a manager who is very tactically astute. Say what you like about their tactics in Copenhagen, Fahy did a great job of isolating our danger men, man-marking them and smothering us completely. Today would be a different kettle of fish, though. Surely he wouldn't be able to outwit us again.

For most of the first half, he did, and if it wasn't for a massive slice of good fortune, he could well have pulled off another tournament victory for the green and gold of Malmö. From the off, John Carroll was a marked man. Aussie Dave, not surprisingly an Australian Rules footballer given his nickname, was designated to follow John all over the park and generally not give him a moment's peace. The pair pulled and dragged and fouled one another from the first whistle as Dave seemed to get the upper hand. Meanwhile Malmö's Iceman, Siggi Josteinsson, was deployed on Niall Scullion to curtail the Antrim man's surges forward in support of our attack. Siggi is another celebrity in Scandinavian Gaelic football circles, and his skill and composure on the ball are a model example for any non-Irish person who tells you they couldn't possibly play this game. Not only would Niall find his route out of defence blocked by Siggi, he would also have his hands full trying to defend against the big Icelandic forward.

Dave's plan was working perfectly. Neither John nor Niall were getting on the ball. Malmö were winning the scrap in midfield, snapping up kick-outs and going on the attack, with Noel Grehan and Michael Lynch sticking a couple of early points on the board for the hosts.

We hit back with a point, but for once it didn't seem like we would be able to pass our way through them or around them. We'd have to go over them and take our chances. Having dominated everyone we met all day, this was something new. In previous games a player under pressure could look to offload the ball to John or Niall, but with both tightly marked we wound up playing around in circles, not getting anywhere.

Then came the hammer blow as Siggi netted a goal. For all their destructive play around the field, Malmö weren't getting the chances they probably deserved until Siggi popped up with his goal. This time it was Malmö who showed their short-passing skills in a dizzying move up their right flank that ended with

Josteinsson slotting home to put Malmö four points ahead. As the roar went up from the home fans crowding the sidelines, the Stockholm defence looked at one another. This wasn't in the script.

John Carroll had had enough. Like many great players, John was more than capable of straying into grey areas when the situation demanded it, and if he was ever going to throw off the human overcoat that was Aussie Dave, it was going to take something special. The two of them had been needling away at each other since the beginning, and now it was time for John to create some space to work.

As the ball broke away from them and they continued to push and pull at one another, John suddenly fell to the ground, pulling Aussie Dave on top of him. We shouted to the referee to attract his attention; from his first glance at the situation, all he could see was John seemingly helpless on the ground with Aussie Dave on top of him and with the Dubliner apparently the victim of an assault by the big Australian. John played the role to perfection. It was a risky strategy but it paid off.

'I've had enough of you pair!' shouted the referee as he reached in his pocket. For a second we thought that both men were going to be sent off for fighting, which would have hurt us more than them. Thankfully, Shay produced a yellow card for each of them and the pendulum swung back in our favour. With his name already in the book and very much on the referee's radar, Dave would have to tread very carefully if he was to avoid being sent off for a second offence. John's plan had worked; Dave would now have to back off a little in his defending, and the smallest chink was all John needed to turn the game around.

Malmö still had the upper hand, but the booking for Dave and a goal from Seán Beatty knocked the stuffing out of them completely. They lost their shape a little and all of a sudden they found themselves outnumbered four to three at the back. The ball was lofted in from the right and after a frenetic scramble Beatty poked home to put us firmly back in the game. It was probably the ugliest goal of the day, beaten only by a second goal for Beatty just before half-time, when he stumbled but somehow still managed to guide the ball into the net. Malmö were down for the count.

The rest of the second half is a blow-out. With Aussie Dave now hamstrung by his booking, John Carroll has the run of the field, and not even a point almost straight from the throw-in for Malmö can convince anyone they can turn it around. Colin lands a beautiful point from the sideline before Declan, Niall and Colin again land three consecutive huge kicks from distance. Like the three-point shot in basketball, a player hitting a point from near the halfway line has a massive effect on both teams: to the conceding team it knocks the stuffing out of them, especially when it's accompanied by the amount of possession that we had; for the scoring team, it lifts them immeasurably. The chests puff out and new reserves of energy are found as the marker is laid down: it doesn't matter how hard you chase, we can score from anywhere.

The Malmö boys are going down with cramp now and the game is interrupted as Seán Beatty helps one of the lads with a tight calf muscle. But whatever mercy or sportsmanship he showed when the ball was out of play disappears the instant the ball comes back in as he heads off on another long, lung-bursting run in search of the third goal that will give him his hat-trick. The tiredness turns the tables. Whereas we were the ones who suffered in Copenhagen, conceding soft frees to hand them victory, now it was the other way round. Drained defenders were forced to drag their men down as they could no longer keep up with them.

Beatty the soccer player might be chasing his hat-trick, but it is John Carroll who comes closest as a high ball in from the right touchline drops short. John has pushed forward from midfield again, and under pressure from the Dubliner who seems to be everywhere all at once, the goalkeeper spills the ball. John pounces to punch home the loose ball, and for us the game is over. With such a commanding lead and only a few minutes left on the clock, I look to the lads on the line and try to catch the attention of Niall or Colin. It's time to clear the bench and give the lads who didn't start a moment in the spotlight.

Incredibly, Shay has disallowed the goal saying that John arrived in the square before the ball. The fact that John dived full length to reach it and fist it home seems to have passed him by. Confusion on the line now; we're still ahead but we're not sure by how far, and even if this Malmö team is out on its feet, no one wants to take a risk. Liam doesn't often concede goals, and the ones he does concede are of the unpredictable variety. A couple of quick flukey strikes could hand the initiative back to our opponents and leave us on the back foot. The reserves have to stay on the line, for now at least.

John Carroll is not done yet. Riled by the fact that he has been denied a goal in the final, he looks determined to put this match to bed once and for all. He runs with the same energy and purpose as he did in our first game of the day four or five hours ago. It's like he's only just shown up and joined in. Another break-up the middle and he puts Ciarán O'Reilly in. The big Cavan man makes no mistake, holding off a heavy challenge and stroking the ball home for the insurance goal we need. Surely there is no way back for Malmö now.

Whatever about Malmö, there's no way back for Ciarán. His knee buckled as he scored and he immediately signals to the sideline that he needs to come off. As in the first game, I tear off my tracksuit top and sprint on to replace him before my name is even called. Again, the moment is a bittersweet one. I'll be on the pitch when the final whistle goes for our first tournament victory, but Ciarán is lying on the ground having an icepack applied to his knee.

I take Ciarán's place up front, and it seems there's a queue of Gaels in the Malmö half of the field, crowding one another to put in their effort to get on the score-sheet in the final. We break forward again and I find John free to my right. Seán is wide open in the middle screaming at him for the ball back, hell-bent on getting his hat-trick, but John takes the shot and slots the ball over the bar. Beatty is livid and I'm not too happy myself. I was free too and would have been delighted to pop one over in the few minutes I had on the pitch. But we're not going to fall out over that now.

The final whistle goes, and a joyous roar goes up from the black-clad Gaels. We've done it. We've come to Malmö and we've won.

The Australian boys with the makeshift bar didn't know what hit them. The lads laughed their way through the warm-down and I sent Karl and Keith off with money to get the first round in, and the party had started. I felt bad about the guys on the line who didn't get a run in the final. As we all gathered in a circle I stressed the fact that every player who had played today had made their contribution to the victory. It was only afterwards I realised that it could have been interpreted as trying to take credit for myself, something that horrified me.

After an hour or so we gathered ourselves together and loaded up the bus to go back, shower, change and get downtown to the prize-giving ceremony. The noise in the hostel was ear splitting as 15 men in dirty football kit sang and danced through the halls in search of towels. It got worse in the showers as the noise echoed off the tiles. I snuck into a cubicle in a corner alone with my thoughts for a second, trying to comprehend the fact that we had won a tournament at last, when a bucket of freezing cold water put a stop to my reverie. But Kevin and Declan, the instigators of this assault, hadn't reckoned on the hosepipe attached to the wall in my cubicle, and seconds later I turned the water cannon on them. Their whoops of joy turned to pain and panic as they realised the water was boiling hot, and I had to switch off the supply as quickly as I could. The singing continued, but the waterworks were finished.

There was no problem getting the lads out and into the bus again for the drive to the pub where the meal would be held. For one thing we were all starving. For another, the few beers the boys had bought for the journey had long since run out and they were desperate for more.

Malmö put on a brilliant buffet spread in a city centre bar and the players from all sides mingled and mixed as they filled their plates and their glasses. Our impression of Malmö has always been that they are kind of like Millwall Football Club in their opinion of themselves, with a 'no one likes us, we don't care' attitude. They didn't hang around in Copenhagen and even when they did socialise, they seemed to want to keep the rest of us at arm's length. But tonight they were fantastic hosts, and all credit to them.

Like all sports Gaelic football is triumphalist, but in its own special way. Score a goal in Gaelic football and you are unlikely to be buried under a mountain of team mates in celebration. You might pump your fist, but that's about it. You then get on with the job in hand. From day one I have stressed the notion of fair play in our club and that if we were ever fortunate enough to be in the position we found ourselves today, we should be as gracious in victory as we had been in defeat.

The clock ticked on towards nine o'clock, and as the World Cup took over the big screens we waited for the trophy to be presented. Captain Carroll in particular was in a hurry to get his hands on the trophy for the simple reason that he and Seán would be taking the overnight bus back to Stockholm. Mark O'Kane had already shot off at the final whistle, racing back to Derry for a family function. Kevin was due to follow him to Ireland the next day, and Seán Beatty was, typically, due to play for his soccer team the following afternoon. If there was no bus back to Stockholm, I'm convinced Beatty would have jogged all the way there.

The presentations and speeches began. Referee Shay was thanked for his participation, and Colin Courtney was given the Player of the Tournament award, although I felt it could have gone to any one of half a dozen of our players, as well as a couple from Malmö and Gothenburg, such was the high standard on show.

Then came the moment we'd all been waiting for as our captain from Armagh went to collect our first club trophy. A livewire bundle of muscles and energy, Kevin Carroll wears his heart on his sleeve, and to hear him speak about what this club and this trophy meant to him made all the effort involved worth it. His honest speech, peppered with the odd swear word here and there, brought massive applause from all present, as well as a few quizzical looks from those from outside Northern Ireland who maybe didn't understand some of his idioms. As he finally raised the trophy in triumph, the Gaels around me went berserk. And I did too.

———

'Ach, sure we'll make it. Will ya have another, Seán?' Kevin has no idea where the bus station is, let alone how long it's going to take him to get there. Seán has a couple of beers and a half-bottle of whiskey in his bag for the long journey up to Stockholm, but neither of them wants to let this moment go. Their day finishes with another lung-bursting run as, full of beer and buffet food, they charge to the bus station to make it just in time for its departure.

For the rest of us staying over, the party is in full swing. The soccer on the TV ends and the DJ starts pumping out the music, and Freddie the Norwegian giant is parading around with Colin's trophy sticking out of the front of his trousers. The cup is filled with beer and shots and passed around all the teams. There will be some sore heads in the morning.

We made sure to get some photographs before Seán and Kevin had to leave, and we make sure to take some more as the night progresses. For some of the participants in the tournament, these may well be the only memories they have after a night on the beer in Malmö.

Around midnight I run up the white flag as the point in the evening approaches where no one is making sense any more. Not only do they end up repeating themselves, I end up repeating myself because they've forgotten what I said five minutes previously. I head back to the hostel for the first sound night's sleep in weeks.

The party continued long into the night, but some are beginning to surface as I get up for breakfast and start packing the van the next morning. The red eyes around the breakfast table are focusing on liquids as the hangovers kick in, and the bag of Barry's teabags has never been more welcome.

Ken Feely is last to be roused from his slumber, having only made it to his bed an hour or two before. He's sitting on his bed, struggling to put his socks on and seemingly having lost the power of speech. As the lads carry his bag and he limps down the stairs I look at him and think to myself, is it all worth it? By Jesus, it is.

We check out of the hostel and hit the road at ten o'clock for another long drive back to Stockholm; but this time it's different.

This time we're bringing the trophy with us, and when we arrive at the Dubliner in about seven hours time, we do so as winners. All the excuses and the injuries and the wounded pride have been replaced by that trophy.

But for all the celebrations, we are back on level terms with Malmö — no more, no less. Our victory yesterday puts us on the same amount of points at the top of the championship table, and judging by the scare they gave us in the first half of the final, there is plenty left to play for. Gothenburg were lurking too, and only a loss to Malmö in their last game prevented them from making the final. If they had done so, the race would have been thrown wide open again, and with two rounds left to play we are only halfway there.

Chapter 10 ∽

A SPORTING CHANCE

Now I know I'm probably slightly more interested in sport than the average man in the street. For one thing I have been writing about it for a living since about midsummer or so.

Ever since I was a kid I have wanted to be a journalist. I have always had a voracious appetite for news. My grandparents lived around the corner from us in Donnycarney, and every evening they would buy the *Evening Press* newspaper and my family would buy the *Evening Herald*. At some point around about eight o'clock one of us would bring our well-thumbed copy of the newspaper around to their house where it would be swapped for the other. That way we got the benefit of reading both newspapers every day. Being Dublin, going to 'bring over the paper' often meant going out in very bad weather, but it wasn't a task that could be avoided. As Alan and I got older and started to read the papers more ourselves, the days when the great Con Houlihan had his column in the *Evening Press* were usually no problem. We always wanted to be first to read him, so we'd fall over each other to volunteer. On those days when Con's byline wasn't featured, volunteers were thin on the ground.

In the 20 years since I left school, it seems I tried everything I could to avoid becoming a journalist. I always enjoyed writing but wasn't sure that the discipline of journalism was something I'd be able to handle. My attitude to studying was similar to my attitude to training. I was lazy to a fault, and it wasn't until my mid-thirties that I realised that arrogance and laziness will only get you so far in life. Nevertheless, when I moved to Sweden I went to work for Reuters; but instead of looking for a job in the newsroom, I started in IT before moving on to marketing. Thomson Reuters (as it is now known) is one of the biggest information companies on the planet, and much of the world's financial system is to some degree dependent on the company and the news and services it provides. By working there I could be part of the culture without necessarily having the responsibility for the news that is produced.

But though I learned a lot about journalism, politics and finance, ultimately it was unsatisfying to watch others do this brilliant work and not be involved myself, so I started to study communications. As time went on I started my own company in the field, and when an opportunity presented itself to become their freelance sports reporter I jumped at it. I had previously spent a lot of time debating the merits of various footballers and tennis players with Oliver Grassman, the previous reporter, and when he moved on to another job it seemed a logical choice for all concerned. I had the knowledge of both how the company worked and of Scandinavian sport, and I was looking for a new challenge. Recognising that there's no point in holding an employee back, I was allowed a leave of absence to see if I could make a go of it. Some would say I'm still trying.

Now that I was self-employed in the realm of sports and communications, I found I had a lot more time over to concentrate on the GAA too. Being surrounded by sport every day gives you a lot of time to reflect on not just why athletes do what they do, but why people react to it and get so carried away with it.

I've come to the realisation that, having watched some form of sport on the telly virtually every day for as long as I can remember, practising a sport yourself is about a thousand times better than watching someone else do it, with very few exceptions. In a major reverse in policy, in the last few years I would much rather go play a game of soccer myself than sit at home and watch a bunch of overpaid divas swan their way through another meaningless Champions League encounter, or another made-for-TV boxing match between two guys more concerned with protecting their good looks than the tattered reputation of their chosen sport. Maybe it's the beginnings of a mid-life crisis, the realisation that my ageing body doesn't have too many more seasons left of blasting balls hopelessly wide of the target. Either way I intend to make the most of it, and though I'm probably a burden to have in any sporting team, as soon as I feel there's no possibility of making a positive contribution, I will take the one course of action which, above all others, has never failed me in my sporting career. I'll quit.

But in those moments when the stars are aligned, there is nothing more beautiful than sport performed at the top level. I've been lucky to meet with and see up close some of the greatest athletes in some of the most popular sports in the world, and it is a privilege. Above all else this is what I seek out in sport: the single breathtaking moment that, win or lose, defines the sport and the sportsman. It could be one of Zlatan's goals; it could be Tyson Gay beating Usain Bolt in the 100 metres; it could be Peter Forsberg's penalty for Sweden. These moments etch themselves instantly in the sporting history books, and I have been lucky to see some of them performed.

Following our maiden victory at the Malmö tournament, there is apparently some mathematical possibility that we could secure the championship at the next tournament in Oslo. I'm pretty doubtful as it will no doubt entail teams not showing up and matches being abandoned due to meteors hitting the pitch or the referee being struck by lightning. Either way, another victory there and we'll be very much in the driving seat with only one tournament to go. But Oslo is going to be a tough one for various reasons.

The main reason is obviously the timing. I don't know how this came to be or who agreed to it or sanctioned it, but the Oslo tournament is due to take place in the middle of July. On the surface it might seem an innocuous enough date for most people, but given that we all live in Scandinavia, they may as well have chosen to play it at midnight on Christmas Day.

It's no secret that Scandinavian countries are among the richest in the world with pretty high standards of living compared to anywhere else. Historians and economists can argue over the reasons for this until the cows come home, but clearly the rising tide has lifted all boats to a certain extent. Workers in Scandinavia, and especially in Sweden, enjoy some of the best and most secure working conditions in the world. It's not unusual for a Swedish worker to have five or six weeks' paid vacation every year (not including bank holidays), and obviously very few people take their days off when the weather is bad in the winter. Add to that the regulations that guarantee every worker the right to take an unbroken three-week break every year and the net result is that the vast majority of people take their holidays sometime between the middle of June and the end of August. Essentially, the country closes down for somewhere between six and eight weeks. And with three of the five clubs competing for the championship based in Sweden, this is going to cause problems, not least for me.

On the surface, the Swedish economy shouldn't really survive such a protracted shutdown, and I'm not really sure how it does. I remember the shock of sending someone an email around midsummer and discovering they wouldn't be back until the beginning of August. I couldn't ever remember having more than a week off at a time in my working life before I moved here, and

I feared that if I ever left the office for that long I would completely forget what my job was in the first place. I can only imagine what it's like for the self-employed. Not only do you have the risk of losing business if you take time off; there's the even bigger risk that you'll have nothing to do if you don't.

Then there are the building and agriculture industries. Now being a Dub, I know nothing of the black arts of farming, which I am more than content to leave to our culchie cousins, and I'm sure the farmers here work just as hard during the summer as their Irish counterparts. But it strikes me as remarkable that the construction industry comes to an almost complete standstill during the very weather in which it could be most productive. Our club covers virtually every profession known to man and there are plenty of tradesmen and construction workers involved, and given the long dark winters here it wouldn't surprise me if they would prefer to work during the balmy summer months and instead head off to somewhere like Thailand in the winter.

The Swedish summer holiday season also represents something of a national gamble for the tourism industry. Whilst the summers here can be absolutely beautiful with long hot days where the sun barely sets, the opposite is also possible. If you're luck isn't in, it can easily compete with the best a wet week in Westport has to offer, minus the great scenery and people of County Mayo. There is little sense in spending a fortune on a sun holiday if the weather is going to be similar — and possibly more pleasant and bearable — in Sweden, so the delivery of holiday brochures in January marks the beginning of a game of cat and mouse between the travel agent, the weatherman and Joe Soap that can go on well into July.

My wife has always lamented my inability to get into the whole idea of taking four or five weeks off and just do nothing. If the truth be told, I find the idea of doing nothing for four or five weeks scary. I need to have something to do, and even if I would be happy to lie on a beach for a couple of days, it has to be with a book. Eventually I'm going to get bored and go buy a football or a basketball and try to find a bunch of equally restless souls to have a game with.

Nor do I buy into the Swedish love of solitude. Given the massive size of this country and the fact that a good deal of it is covered in forest, there are plenty of opportunities to withdraw to a cabin and just be by yourself. My father-in-law's family come from a small village 500 kilometres north of Stockholm, where the people are not only used to such isolation, they actually appear to enjoy it. But the very notion of heading to the cabin he and his brother still own up there fills me with dread.

A stone's throw from our apartment in Stockholm we have a shopping centre with hundreds of shops, restaurants and bars and an 11-screen cinema. There are football pitches and basketball courts and playgrounds dotted around the place like confetti, and a metro station from which you can get to the heart of one of the most modern and beautiful cities in Europe in 15 minutes and enjoy all it has to offer. There are Irish pubs and football matches and concerts and museums and zoos and people we know. And if that fails there is an international airport 20 minutes in the other direction that would soon take you to wherever it is you want to go.

At the father-in-law's cabin in Hedeviken, within sight of the border between Sweden and Norway, there is nothing. The local shops close at teatime, and if you haven't got what you need for the weekend by about two o'clock on Saturday, you won't be getting it till Monday — that's if they have it at all. The biggest tourist attraction is a stuffed bear in the lobby of one of the local buildings. Apparently the bear wandered into the village one day and was shot by the locals. I find that disturbing for two reasons: for one thing, there was so little to do or eat in the area that a creature as notoriously shy as a bear was forced to enter civilisation, driven by hunger and fear and loneliness. That says everything to me about the area in general. Even more disturbing is the fact that as soon as the locals got wind of the new and exciting visitor in town, they tooled themselves up and shot him. I made a mental note to keep my suave Dublin wit to myself, lest I meet a similar fate — shot, stuffed and on display at the Hedeviken post office, dressed in a Dubs tracksuit with a look of utter boredom on my face.

To be fair, when I said there was nothing there, I was bending the truth a little; there is cold running water in the kitchen of the cabin, as well as billions and billions of mosquitoes and gnats during the summer.

But the father-in-law loves it and if his wife agreed he'd probably live there. He loves the solitude and nature and the idea of chopping down a tree and making a stool or a coffee table. He thinks nothing of heading off at dawn — which in the summer is around two in the morning — and going deep into the forest to the lake where he keeps his rowing boat. He can sit there for the day with a flask of coffee and some sandwiches, completely cut off from the outside world. If he catches something, he'll bring it home and cook it for dinner. If not, he's not bothered.

The people who live year round in such circumstances are hardy, resourceful and stoic. Temperatures during the winter can get down below -30, and darkness lies over the area like a blanket for months at a time, broken only by the reflection of the moon and the stars and the few street lights on the snow.

Much of the work available is seasonal, agriculture in the summer and work at the ski resorts in the winter providing much of the employment. Hunting, fishing and wild fruits, berries and vegetables provide much of what ends up on the dinner table, and a snow scooter in this part of the world is more a necessity than a status symbol. In short, it's the kind of place in which Dublin people like me should never be left unaccompanied.

Even if I find it hard to understand why the Swedes would risk spending thousands for guaranteed sun during the summer, I'm sure they find our annual family holiday plans just as odd, and probably as big a waste of money. One of the conditions of living abroad, especially since our children were born, is that we spend part of our family holiday in Ireland every year as well as every second Christmas. When the rest of Sweden is waiting for the holiday brochures to hit the mat in January, the Irish community is spending hours online to find the best deal to bring a family of four with two pieces of luggage to check in to Dublin and beyond in July. Everyone is aware of the restrictions and conditions when flying with Ryanair, but given the expense of flying four people to Ireland a couple of times a year, sometimes it's worth the hassle.

For our partners, it's one of the many trade-offs they have to make for getting involved with an Irish person. Instead of spending these ten days or two weeks in a cabin in the middle of nowhere, or on a beach in Greece, we drag them off to Ireland where the unpredictability of the weather is only matched by the unpredictability of our families. Often grown men and women find themselves sharing their parents' family home many years after they left it, and given the intensity of Irish family life, it's a wonder the Swedes survive it at all.

To make it easier for all concerned, we usually spend a couple of days in Galway or Belfast, allowing everyone the chance for some breathing room. It's no harm for the kids to get away either, as they are often dragged around and put on display as if they were exhibits in some sort of freak show. Massive doses of late nights coupled with foods they would never be allowed to eat at home are usually not the best combination either, and often they need a couple of days of rest when they get back to Sweden, exhausted after being immersed in Ireland and Irish culture for their summer holidays.

But these are important visits for them too. They are

surrounded by people who talk and act like their mum or dad, and behaviour that would be seen as being odd in Sweden is perfectly acceptable. They get to see the places their parents come from, the streets and fields they played in and where they went to school. And as the children get older there are no more popular summer day trips than nostalgic wanderings around a parent's home town. The voices and accents on the radio and the television are oddly familiar, and music of one form or another is never too far away.

Then there is the sport. Summer in Ireland would be nothing without the pilgrimages to Croke Park and Páirc Uí Chaoimh, Semple Stadium and Casement Park. The headlines and the airwaves buzz with previews as the titans clash on a Saturday or a Sunday, and in the following week the games are dissected in all their detail, starting at the final whistle. There are club games and training sessions and cúl camps and the rest, and kids with hurls and kitbags bigger than themselves wander the streets. Summer evenings are spent on the sidelines watching the up and coming player of tomorrow as the endless calendar of the GAA season shifts shape once more to allow for some unforeseen circumstance. And around all these players and coaches are the hundreds of mentors, supporters and officials, the people whose lives in some way orbit their club or county team. These are the kind of people who are first in the queue at the office in Dorset Street when the tickets go on sale for Dublin against Louth in the first round of the championship. Even though it wouldn't sell out in a million years, that is not the point. This is who they are and this is what they do. Hopefully witnessing all of this goes some way towards explaining why their mammies and daddies spend their time and money travelling the length and breadth of Scandinavia in the hope of bringing home a trophy or a medal that the whole family can be proud of.

With all this in mind, I thought it made perfect sense. As usual the family holiday to Ireland had been booked months in advance for the middle of July and would coincide nicely with my mother's birthday and my parents' wedding anniversary. A trip up to Belfast and the Giant's Causeway was pencilled in, as was a quick visit to Galway to visit friends there too. But all this was before Oslo decided to put their tournament in the Scandinavian holiday wasteland that is the middle of July.

So it seemed only natural to me that I'd have to consider a quick flight to Oslo for the tournament. If the gods of air travel were willing and the timetables could be believed, I'd only be out of Ireland for about 48 hours or so, and 36 wasn't beyond the bounds of possibility. All I would need was hand luggage and a Ryanair flight to Oslo, where Pat Walker, a Carlow man and coach of the professional soccer side Sandefjord, could collect me and whizz me off to the tournament. Pat has spent most of his adult life working in Scandinavia as a professional footballer and soccer coach, and I have known him for a few years. He'd love to spend a day at a Gaelic football tournament, and with that as the carrot I was sure he'd oblige. From there we'd hopefully do the business as we had in Malmö, at which point I'd hotfoot it back to the airport and head back to Dublin. The worst-case scenario would be that I would have to go via Stansted. Surely Maria and the kids wouldn't mind?

The discussion with my wife didn't go exactly as I had planned, and looking back I made a couple of rookie errors. I'm sure she was well aware of how important this club and this team had become to me, and how the quest for the Scandinavian championship had become all the more intense since our resounding victory in Malmö. But somewhere along the line I neglected to explain what was in it for her; in fairness, that might be because there was very little, and the little there was in it for her was mostly negative. She would be left in Ireland with the kids by herself for a couple of days whilst I was off chasing my dreams around a football field in the capital of Norway. A suggestion that she could spend this time in Longford with our ex-flatmate and one of our best friends, Bronwyn, met with the same frosty silence as the rest of my arguments. I must admit I thought it was strange, but I hadn't quite given up hope.

Bronwyn would have understood. Her partner Malcolm was a former class mate of mine back in Ardscoil Rís, a fanatical hurler whose talent for the game matched his interest in it. Malcolm was always a very straightforward black-and-white guy, on and off the pitch. There weren't too many grey areas with him, and if you lined up alongside him on a football or hurling field you knew exactly what you were going to get. Their son Oisín had a hurl put in his hand from the time he could grip a spoon and was already playing mini-leagues and camps with the Fingallions club near their home in Swords. If it wasn't for the pressures of work and family life I think Malcolm would still be playing hurling himself. Whatever he lacks in fitness he could surely make up quickly, and the class a hurler like him has is permanent.

It might have seemed like an indecent proposal, but I was sure Maria would understand why the idea had popped into my head. That I was interested in sport was nothing new to her; indeed when we met in Dublin in 1994, she was a Swedish au pair in Dublin. The soccer World Cup in America that year took place shortly after we met, and though it is fondly remembered in Ireland for Ray Houghton's fantastic goal and our opening victory against Italy, the Swedes took themselves all the way to the semi-finals, where they lost by the odd goal to Brazil before hammering Bulgaria 4-0 in the third-place play-off. From the very beginning of our relationship she was aware of what sport meant to me.

Fast-forward to our wedding plans for 2002 and they almost all went west. We had chosen Friday 21 June as our wedding date, being midsummer's eve and probably the most important holiday in the Swedish calendar alongside Christmas Day. But again the World Cup was under way and a quick look at the fixtures showed there was a good possibility that Ireland could end up playing on the morning of our wedding day. Now, being an Irish man interested in sport doesn't exactly make me unique, and the prospect of the Irish contingent spending the morning of our wedding in some bar cheering on their heroes wasn't all that appealing to the bride-to-be or her family. I'll have to be honest and say I found it an intriguing possibility, which is yet more evidence of the fundamental differences in our approaches to life and sport. As it was, the Irish had their morning in the sun anyway, as Ronaldinho lobbed David Seaman to send England crashing out of the World Cup. Not only was it the happiest day of my life, it was the happiest day that many of those in attendance could remember, more on account of Ronaldinho than me.

Even if my old man is fanatically interested in sport, I don't think the blame for fostering my obsession is his to bear alone. There is no doubt I learned much of what I know about sport from him, but the chances are I would have turned out pretty similar no matter what Irish family I grew up in. Watching sport is such a huge part of life in Ireland and few families remain unaffected by it. Golfers tend to produce golf fanatics, football lovers tend to produce football fanatics, and if anyone ever bothered to study it, there is probably evidence that a love of rugby is genetic. Indeed, most Irish people are in no way exclusive or snobbish when it comes to sport. Sports like golf and rugby might be considered elitist in other countries, but they are almost working class in Ireland. Whatever about rugby and the rest, Gaelic football and hurling are weaved into the DNA of most Irish people.

My sporting interests and obsessions are of a different nature to my dad. The only son in a family of three children, he was born in 1945 into a working-class family, the father from the village of Rathmore and the mother from Clare. It would be easy to think that the role of the athlete was foisted on him because he was the only son, but his younger sister Ann is just as interested, if not more so. Virtually all the stories my father ever told me about his upbringing had something to do with sport. It was both his compass and his calendar; he could find his way around the country only because he knew the counties and clubs through football and hurling. If a town didn't have a stadium of a certain size or a county championship club, he would bypass it. In much the same way I would tell people I met my wife just before the World Cup in 1994, every event in his life was pegged to a sporting event. It was simpler to turn history and geography into one subject and learn that instead. That subject was called sport.

In the seventies he used the geographical knowledge gained from the wireless and the back pages of the newspapers to haul us over the country as he followed what many viewed as the hopeless quest of the Dublin footballers for All-Ireland glory. Never a smoker or a drinker, he didn't frequent pubs, but he still managed to get into arguments at the counter of the local builder provider's where he went to buy the materials to keep his building company running. There he would give the fair-weather fans stick for only ever turning up for the later rounds of the championship, whilst he and the handful of other true believers would travel the length and breadth of the country closely studying the progress of Brian Mullins and the rest. Of course, in the end he was proved right as the Dubs won the All-Ireland, but instead of enjoying that moment for which he had waited for years, he seemed to fall out of love with Gaelic football. The weekday evenings at Parnell Park and the Sunday trips to Croke Park became more and more infrequent, and by the time the Dubs were done getting hammered by Kerry in the 1985 final, he was more or less done with them altogether and seldom if ever seen in Croke Park.

His dedication to the cause of Irish rugby was also legendary in our household, and nothing could frustrate him more than an insipid or uninspiring performance from an Irish rugby team, until an Irish golfer called Philip Walton came along. Walton was a ridiculously talented amateur from Malahide, and to this day I still don't know why my father took him on board, but for years he would be glued to the lunchtime sports news on RTÉ Radio to find out how Walton's opening round had gone at whatever tournament the European Tour were playing that week. This would be followed by regular updates until Sunday evening, by which time the outcome of the whole tournament would be known. In the days before the internet, every snippet of information gleaned from the radio, the newspapers or text TV was treated almost like gold dust.

When the Irish Open took place he would take the Thursday and the Friday off and for the four days religiously follow Walton around the 72 holes he would hopefully get to play. I used to go with him and enjoyed collecting the autographs of the star players like Greg Norman and Nick Faldo, but my father had no interest in meeting or talking to Walton; instead, he would follow him around the course, studying him quietly and intently. At that time qualification for the Ryder Cup was decided by how much prize money a player won on the tour, and in the run-up to the Ryder Cup my father would know more about Walton's earnings than he would about his own. When he did finally make the team in 1995, Walton famously won the match that clinched the Ryder Cup for Europe. Like the Dubs winning the All-Ireland football final, it marked a cooling in my father's interest in the golfer from Malahide. He still followed his progress, but there was no longer the desperate scramble for the four-day pass to follow Walton around Portmarnock or Royal Dublin.

Like every kid on the northside, my first sporting heroes were the Dublin Gaelic footballers and in particular Kevin Moran. Moran's move from Dublin to Manchester United was one of the defining moments for a generation of young sports fans. Though there were still those in the GAA who hated soccer and all it stood for and vice versa, Moran's crossing the line made the position of many of them untenable. I didn't love Kevin Moran any less because he had gone to Manchester United and left the Dubs behind; in fact I loved him more, and now the whole world, or at least the English part of it, would get to see my hero in action. That he was the first man to be sent off in an FA Cup final was simple proof of a conspiracy against Irish heroes in English sport: Moran was so superior they had to send him off to stop him imposing himself on the game.

Soccer was tremendously exciting, and the colour and noise beamed into our homes from the 1978 World Cup captivated me for life. I'm not sure if it was deliberate or not, but my father never had an allegiance towards any particular English team. Even if he would watch whatever games were shown on television, it was never apparent who he wanted to win.

I flirted with many clubs, mostly because of an Irish connection, and I always had a lot of respect for the likes of Liverpool, Arsenal and Manchester United because of their Irish contingents. Of all the clubs in England, my favourite would be Newcastle United; partially because of the wonderful people of the north-east, but also because they were once home to great Irish players like Liam O'Brien, David Kelly and Kevin Sheedy. Players like Moran going to Sporting Gijon and Frank Stapleton going to Ajax were impossibly brilliant to me. That these Dubliners who grew up playing football on the same kind of streets that I played on could be successful abroad was proof to me of our collective greatness. We might come from a poor country on the edge of Europe, and the headlines on the front pages may have preached poverty and unemployment and the death of hope for generations to come, but if we turned over the pages and saw Liam Brady strutting his stuff for Juventus we were reassured that it was possible for us to claim our place in the world.

The world of basketball was also fascinating to me. I've always been tall, and even before my focus shifted from Gaelic football to basketball I had got caught up in the magic of Larry Bird and the Boston Celtics and their perennial clashes with Magic Johnson and the LA Lakers. I was immediately sold on the name, and to see big Irish-looking guys like Bird, Kevin McHale and Danny Ainge go toe to toe with the glitzy showtime players of the Lakers and win was the stuff of dreams for me. I had Bird pegged as the all-American hero, the guy who could do no wrong. I later found out that he was one of the biggest trash-talkers in the game, taking every opportunity to abuse his opponents and undermine their confidence.

If I had known that at the time, I would probably have dropped him like a stone. I wanted my sporting heroes to be just that — sporting. It wasn't enough for them to be athletic and creative and gifted, capable of things that normal men and women could only dream of; they had to be pure of spirit as well. In 1982 I was immensely proud of the achievements of the Northern Ireland soccer team in getting to the World Cup finals and giving such a great account of themselves. I was too young and ignorant to understand the political implications of why the island had two national teams; I was just delighted to see fellas like Gerry Armstrong — himself a former Gaelic footballer — scoring goals against the mighty Spain at the world's favourite tournament.

In this raw and intrusive era where we know every little detail and snatch of gossip about our heroes, we can no longer fool ourselves that they are anything other than human. Before the dawn of the internet, the paparazzi and 24-hour rolling news services we could still convince ourselves that our heroes weren't only brilliant on the field, but they never drank, smoked or swore, and they always gave up their seat to an old person on the bus. It must be so much harder for kids to have idols today when we know from the off that they are only human like us.

Towards the end of the 1980s, girls and alcohol took a temporary grasp of our attention, but soccer and Gaelic games were never too far from our minds. The advent of Jack Charlton saved us from the sporting wilderness, and in dragging us to the European Championship finals in Germany in 1988 and the World Cup for the very first time two years later, he put Ireland on the map like never before. The older lads I grew up with on the streets in Donnycarney were also sporting herbivores who would consume anything that came their way. Sundays would see Anto Savage head off down the road to the Hill 16 terrace at Croke Park, following in the footsteps of generations of family members before him. It was through him I learned that Bohemians FC were the soccer team of choice in our area and I dutifully started to follow their results in the evening papers. Not too many people took the bus from Whitehall church down Dorset Street towards Dalymount Park to watch them and it was deemed too dangerous a place for me to go on my own. Besides, wasn't soccer full of hooligans anyway? That most of these self-same hooligans would also frequent Croke Park was never mentioned. I couldn't wait to be old enough to go to all these sporting Meccas by myself.

So I was somewhat surprised when Maria didn't seem too keen on the idea of me taking off in the middle of our family holiday to go and play in the Oslo tournament, and I was even more taken aback when the word 'divorce' was mentioned. Never the sort of girl to make threats lightly, I could see that obviously this wasn't something that was on the table for negotiation. Not yet.

With the standard of players we had in our club we'd be confident of beating anyone, but the squad was looking a little threadbare as the tournament approached. Most of the lads with families were in the same predicament as me, hamstrung by circumstance. I vowed not to make the same mistake again, and next year the family holiday might well include a camping trip that happens to coincide with one of the regional rounds.

The single lads were once again our salvation. They didn't have Swedish women polluting their minds with thoughts of time off to be spent doing nothing in some wilderness, and as it happened, many of them worked for Irish or UK companies who had a totally different rhythm when it came to summer holidays. Most of them wouldn't be looking to go anywhere until the first two weeks in August, by which time Scandinavia would be starting to wake up from its summer slumber. With many of the city's best bars and nightclubs either empty or closed down, they would welcome the chance for a weekend away at a tournament to relieve the boredom. Among them were the hard core from the previous summer. Colin, Mark and Ken would all travel, as would the Sundbyberg Express. Stalwarts like Niall Balfe and Barry Quinn were signed up to play in the forward line; John Carroll had somehow managed to wangle his way out of the house for the weekend, and Seán Beatty would be escaping the summer heat in the underground kitchen of the Dubliner to take part. Keith Hearne would make his second appearance; having missed the first tournament in Copenhagen, his presence was absolutely crucial now.

The ever-faithful Liam was up for a stint in goal; by now he'd managed to establish with his employer that one weekend a month off wasn't asking too much, even if he did work in the catering business, and it seemed to me if he put his foot down he could have got even more time off. They needed him more than he needed them. Chefs of that quality don't grow on trees.

Nigel O'Reilly was making a comeback too, having missed the Malmö victory, and to cap it all Phil Cahill would be making the trip. Finally we would have someone on the sideline to take the pressure off Niall and Colin and let them get on with their own game. They had done a great job but understood the limitations when trying to coach and play at the same time.

That Phil would be the one to take over was a massive bonus. We had long discussed nominating someone — virtually anyone — to the role and basically giving them a set of key instructions with regard to substitutions and who should go on to play where, when changes should be made, and so on. The man on the sideline would also be the touch point for all communication with the coaches on the field, passing on messages to players and relating things back to them.

With Phil travelling none of this would be necessary. Anything any of us could tell Phil, he knew already. An inter-county player for Meath in both hurling and football, he had coached both codes before moving to Sweden to work for Ericsson. Phil is one of the few Meath men I've met who places hurling above football in the pantheon of Irish sport, but he is not one of those hurlers that would burst every football in the county. Hurling only shades it in his affections. Either way, his encyclopaedic knowledge of Gaelic games and fitness training will prove to be massive assets for us in the second half of the season.

But unless he's also a qualified marriage guidance counsellor, he won't be able to do much to help my participation. Even though Colin is worried that we'll only have the bare bones of a squad going to Oslo, there's seemingly nothing I can do to get away from Dublin to the tournament. I'm already in trouble because I'll have to cover a tennis tournament for the news agency whilst on holiday, so I decide to keep my mouth shut. Still, I hide a pair of boots and my shorts and socks at the bottom of my suitcase just in case the emergency call comes through and I have to hotfoot it to Oslo to make up the numbers.

It's not just wanting to play that is the problem. The idea that the club will be taking part in such an important tournament and I won't be there in any capacity is not sitting well with me for a number of reasons. I might have been the one to forget the kit on the trip to Malmö, but it made it in the end, as did the video camera, spare tapes, batteries, medical kit, cones, bibs, sunscreen and hundreds of other small items that the team needs when it goes on the road. We have been documenting the whole season so far using a video camera borrowed from an old school friend who now lives on the southside of Stockholm, but if I'm not there I doubt there'll be a whole lot of footage coming out of the Oslo tournament. I wouldn't feel good about lending it out and not being there to take responsibility for it. Besides, if we don't have enough players, there's every chance it will be left unused in its bag on the sideline.

I won't be there to update the Twitter feed either, so it looks like my participation will be limited to checking for updates on Karl Lambert's Facebook page as the day progresses. Karl is a naturally sociable character and his updates to the thousand or so friends he has on Facebook are the stuff of legend by now. Unusually for him, he is quiet around the tournaments, or at least around the parts of them played on the field. I'm not sure it's because he feels he doesn't have the same level of experience as some of the other lads, because that hardly makes a difference; watching the Sundbyberg Express win the ball and stride forward purposefully into midfield, you'd swear he was born to play centre back for Wicklow.

In the run-up, the news for the other clubs doesn't get any better. Copenhagen won't have the numbers to travel, and in the days before the tournament Billy is forced to run up the white flag. Gothenburg won't make it either. But regardless of how many teams there are, there are still the same amount of championship points to be played for, and for ourselves and

Malmö fighting it out at the top of the table, this tournament is getting more and more crucial. Both sides will be weakened. The question is how much, and who will be able to hang on for victory.

With only three teams taking part, the time pressure disappears and the first game isn't due to start until midday. By this time I'm in Dublin pulling my hair out waiting for updates, but none is forthcoming. Finally, the text arrives: everyone is good to go and the games will be extended to 30 minutes. That means that once again 90 minutes of football will be required to win the final.

For once, it's our turn to open the tournament against the hosts. The draw has been kind to us, pitting us first against Oslo and then Malmö before a break as those two play each other. All going well, we'll meet the winner of that game in the final. That said, the Gaels won't be taking anything for granted.

Which proves to be the right approach. Oslo are the home team and common sense would say that the home team should always be at its strongest. They have come a long way since they had to borrow Kieran from Copenhagen to make up the numbers in the first tournament a few short months ago, and there are at least four or five new faces in their line-up. As referee Mike Cryan throws the ball up to start the game, one of these new faces beats John Carroll and Niall to the jump. He hits the ground, takes a step and bangs the ball over the bar from the halfway line. Niall looks at John, and then back at the posts. Fuck, he thinks. Did that just happen?

So much for the weakest team in the tournament. It's backs to the wall stuff as Oslo go all out to prove that on their day they can match anyone else in the region. Freddie is doing his usual mad Viking act, thundering around the field, and one late tackle gives John Carroll a dead leg. John limps on until half-time, but eventually he's forced to give up and take over the goalkeeping duties from Liam. The soft-spoken Clare man finds himself thrust into the fray in midfield alongside Niall.

But there is worse to come. After several tournaments where his over-physical nature has gone unpunished, Freddie finally causes a serious injury. Niall Balfe's tidy, clever play has made him a go-to guy off the bench for the Gaels, and his 'get it, give it and go' approach has meant plenty of playing time as we sought to close out games or take the sting out of an opponent that was getting too frisky. From the left half back position Niall takes control of the ball and sees Freddie bearing down on him. Niall loops the ball over the lumbering Norwegian and the Gaels are on the attack again. But Freddie doesn't bother slowing down and crashes straight into him, dislocating Niall's shoulder. The latest in a long line of petulant, pointless fouls has ended not just this tournament for the affable Dubliner, but most likely his whole season.

The news reaches me in Dublin and I'm raging. It has been obvious from day one that this was going to happen, and neither his own players nor the referees have taken enough action to nip it in the bud. I think back to the very first game we played against them, when Freddie kicked out at Mark as the Derry man glided past him. Maybe if John Kelleher had shown him the line for that one, Niall wouldn't be lying in the dirt in Oslo with his shoulder out of its socket. I think back to my own experience of marking him, where I received the ball in front of him and he beat me like a drum. Again, he went unpunished. And when he shouldered me in the back as I shaped to shoot, I was close to losing my temper with the referee once again. It seemed that Oslo were entitled to do whatever they wanted. Sure, they had a tough time of it and had been on the end of a few heavy beatings, but the way to drag themselves up by the bootstraps was to start taking their chances, not putting guys out of the game completely. At the end of the day we are all amateurs and come Monday morning the majority of us have jobs to go to. Anyone deliberately or recklessly injuring another player is taking bread off that man's table, and I can't think of anything worse.

Of course, the biggest responsibility is with Freddie himself, and in truth we need characters like him if we are to grow the games here. But not at any price. It is up to his club mates and the referees to help him with his behaviour. It's a shame that a guy who has contributed so much to his club off the field can do so much damage to its reputation on it.

That single point scored from the throw-in was to prove their only score. John Carroll played Niall in for a goal soon afterwards and the Gaels were back on top. Tails lifted after Niall's injury and the late tackle on John Carroll, there was to be no fairytale ending to this game for the Norwegians, and Colin even had the luxury of a missed penalty in the first half. When Niall clipped over a sideline ball off the outside of his right boot in the second half, the writing was on the wall.

The watching Malmö side must have been relishing their chances. Stockholm had been through one of the toughest 30 minute games of the season, and now the bench was cleared. There were no more substitutes to turn to, and the talismanic John Carroll had had to retreat into goal. The lads from Skåne had every reason to believe that if they were going to breathe life back into this championship, now was the time to do it.

Another ding-dong match followed. Malmö were also weakened by absent players, but their high-tempo pressing game is not dependent on any one individual, and they put it up to Stockholm from the throw-in. Both sides chipped away at each other in a tough, physical encounter, but neither could really gain the upper hand. I got a message at half-time: 'On top, can't put them away.'

One aspect of team sports that never fails to surprise me is that it throws up the most unlikely heroes. When the chips are down and the star players are having trouble, it takes a player of great character to step up and grab the game by the scruff of the neck and drag it off in the right direction. Barry Quinn from Carlow might not be the most natural footballer, but he is as strong as an ox and virtually impossible to knock off the ball. He might cough it up to you, but you're not going to go in there and take it. An injury kept him out of the action in Malmö, but if the Copenhagen tournament was anything to go by, he would have to resign himself to periods on the bench, even in Oslo. But the injury to Niall changed all that and he now had a key role in the forward line, holding up the ball, buying time, making space and generally keeping the opposition backline under pressure. And just when his team were struggling and needed him most, he turned and fired home to break the back of Malmö's challenge and set Stockholm up for a third final in three tournaments.

Barry's goal did more than just beat Malmö: by winning our second game it set us up for the final against whoever emerged victorious from the next game. Barry's strike had forced Malmö to up the tempo and chase the game and now, deflated and exhausted by a third straight defeat by us and badly in need of a rest, they had to face a hungry home side that scented blood, whilst we looked on from the sidelines.

Not being there, I thought the result texted to me in Dublin was a mistake. Had Oslo really knocked half a dozen goals past Malmö? Were we really going to meet them in the final, with our biggest rivals in the tournament watching us from the sideline? Incredibly we were.

Sensing that their moment of glory had come, and well rested after their opening defeat by us, Oslo tore into Malmö from the start. With home advantage and the availability of their best players, they showed no mercy to a tired Malmö side, knocking a hatful of goals past them as they joyously barged their way into their first final in a regional tournament. If it was a boxing match the referee would have stopped it early in the second half. The Oslo players kept coming in, wave after wave, all desperate to play their part in their historic first victory on home turf. Come what may, this victory would be celebrated tonight and for many nights to come.

A shell-shocked Malmö were out. Instead of facing a short rest and a third straight game on an intense afternoon, they would be running the sidelines and doing the umpiring at a final that no one would have predicted that morning. I'm not too sure that Malmö would have relished a third straight game in such circumstances. It's virtually impossible to keep up the pace and intensity required by Gaelic football for 90 straight minutes, and in the heat of the Oslo summer I have a feeling they might just have wilted even further when faced with a Stockholm side that had rested for an hour. But all that was hypothetical now.

Oslo rode the wave of euphoria into the final itself and the first few minutes were nip and tuck as the Norwegians' new-found confidence gave them almost superhuman powers. They had scored more in the game against Malmö than in the whole season to date and, conscious that this chance may not come around again in a hurry, they were eager to grab it with both hands. Again, Stockholm would have to find a moment of brilliance to break the deadlock, and again Freddie's lack of discipline would let his side down.

Just as the Dutch masters of Total Football could adjust and play in any position on the pitch, we are lucky to have players who can fit in anywhere and do a job. The likes of Kevin Carroll, Ken Feely and Mark O'Kane could walk into any football team, pull on a shirt and not look out of place no matter where the coach put them. Niall Scullion had played in virtually every position for us so far this season at one time or another, and even though Colin Courtney's talents were best deployed at full forward, his speed and technique meant he could also play at midfield or half forward to devastating effect.

So it was Niall, nominally a midfielder in the final, who found himself chasing down the Oslo corner back as Stockholm turned up the pressure on the hosts. The Antrim man dived in to block the attempted clearance, but instead of getting a clean block the ball got stuck between his arms and he came away with it. Realising he had the defence on the back foot, he fired the ball inside to Courtney, who bore down on goal intent on opening up a gap to build on. Freddie had other ideas and came barging into the area to drag Colin down. Referee Mike Cryan was left with no choice. A penalty for Courtney and a red card for Freddie. The only thing unusual about his sending-off was that it had taken until his tenth game for a referee to send him to the line.

Courtney made no mistake from the penalty spot, and though the Gaels would struggle on until half-time without opening up a big lead, the game was up. Even with home advantage and their best players on show, Oslo weren't going to be able to come back from being a man down and five or six points behind. They had given their all against Malmö, tearing forward in search of more goals even when the game was well out of sight. How they must have wished they had conserved some of that energy as Keith Hearne buried the ball in the back of the net in the second half to give Stockholm an unassailable lead and virtually hand us our second tournament victory in a row. Mike blew the final whistle and the Gaels collapsed in joyous exhaustion, delighted to emerge with a victory from what was a potential banana skin.

But the physical wounds would take longer to heal. Niall Balfe's dislocated shoulder would keep him out for months to come, and as the team headed to the harbour in the centre of Oslo for the prize-giving ceremony and a few drinks, another serious injury occurred. It was bad enough having John Carroll crocked with a dead leg, but as the evening wore on Niall Scullion also had to cut the festivities short as a shoulder injury sustained during the day was getting progressively worse. The more people came over and slapped him on the back to congratulate him, the worse it got, and eventually he headed back to the hostel early to avoid doing any more damage.

Despite a second tournament victory and stretching our unbeaten run, it was still tight at the top of the table. Malmö picked up 16 points for their third place, which meant we would have to make the final in the last round of the Gothenburg tournament to be sure of winning the championship. This one was going right down to the wire, but with injuries and other commitments the cracks in our squad were beginning to show.

Kevin's family situation meant that while he would most likely travel, you could never be a hundred per cent sure until you actually got him on the bus. Then there was the risk of a player getting injured in training. We already knew John Carroll would be back in Dublin and that Ciarán's knee wasn't going to be better in time. Now, as a result of this latest shoulder injury, we were limping towards the final round with the championship within our grasp. Can we hold our squad together?

Chapter 11

MONEY'S TOO TIGHT TO MENTION

Colin and I are in our suits in the bank at lunchtime. The bank manager disappeared with a fistful of freshly signed papers half an hour ago and hasn't come back yet. We're wondering if he's simply given up. Maybe it's just not worth the bother of getting involved with some Irish sporting organisation, especially when they come in here and cause this much hassle.

If I am an unlikely choice as chairman, then Courtney is the perfect treasurer. His mastery of Excel means there is no equation too complex for him, and the fact that he remained unfazed by tax law in a foreign language was almost enough for me to propose that he become treasurer for life.

No sooner had the club been formed than we needed money. Training facilities had to be paid for, balls and jerseys and medical stuff had to be bought, and we had to have some way of collecting membership fees and the various monies necessary to take part in tournaments and competitions. In the beginning some of us gave our membership fees to Colin in cash, or we simply bought stuff out of our own pockets and didn't bother asking for the money back. But as time went on and more and more members started to join, we needed to get ourselves organised. We had been careful to set ourselves up properly and register as a sporting organisation so that we would stay on the right side of the authorities. At first the tax office rejected our application for sporting status as we hadn't included the minutes of the meeting that founded the club, or of the first AGM. It seemed a bit petty to us, but then it was these meetings that gave the club its legitimacy under Swedish law — a nod and a wink wouldn't be enough.

The documents were dug up and the application resubmitted, only to be denied again. This time we had submitted the minutes of the meeting in English, which of course wasn't acceptable. We would have to translate the documents and go through the whole process again.

For a country with a fluency in English that is better than most, the Swedes have an odd relationship to the language. English is introduced to the school curriculum at the age of 8 or 9, and a steadfast refusal to dub TV programmes into Swedish means children are exposed to it from a very early age. But the Swedes are not a boastful people; most of them tend to play down their knowledge of the English language, claiming it to be less than what it is. The same people could probably read the entire works of Joyce without ever opening a dictionary. Paradoxically, when they have a few drinks they are more than happy to converse in English, at the very time when the ability to speak it tends to desert them. They are not alone in this: many Irish people aren't much use at speaking any language after ten pints either.

But if they wanted the minutes in Swedish we would be more than happy to oblige, and they were duly translated and proofread before the paperwork was submitted for a third and, thankfully, final time. We were — legally at any rate — a sporting organisation with the papers to prove it.

A visit to Swedbank in the centre of Stockholm was arranged. I wasn't sure this was such a good idea. Colin and a handful of the other lads worked as consultants for them a stone's throw away; if they'd known that, they probably wouldn't have let us in the door.

But just because they put bread on his table doesn't guarantee our new bank manager an easy ride, and it's not long before Colin's gentle but firm line of questioning has him pulling uncomfortably at his collar. He's trying to sell us a package of services like online bookkeeping and credit cards linked to the club accounts, but Courtney is having none of it. 'What does it cost? No, we don't need that.'

I start to almost feel sorry for the guy and feel like throwing him a bone, but instead I sit back and enjoy the spectacle. Courtney has given plenty of corner backs the runaround this season, so it's fun to watch him do it in a suit.

Then it comes to the payments and who is going to sign for what and how. The bank manager insists on giving us two of those little electronic devices that spit out codes to be used when banking online. 'Oh, that's grand,' I say. 'We'll only need the one for Colin.'

'That's not how it works,' says the bank manager. 'You have to have two of them.'

'But we don't want two.'

'But you have to have them.'

'OK. Colin, you can take mine as well. I have too many of these fecking things at home.'

'You can't do that!' says the bank manager, exasperated.

'Why not?'

'You need to be able to log in and check the balances, to make sure he's doing his job and no money is going missing!'

'There's not that much money to begin with, chief. And besides, I know where he lives.'

The bank manager gathers up the papers in a fluster and leaves the room to make some copies. Colin and I smile. That put a stop to his gallop.

Money is rife in sport. On some days in the newspapers, if it wasn't for the pictures you could be forgiven for thinking that you'd opened the business pages instead of the sports pages. The headlines speak of contracts and terms and wages and commercial sponsorship. No longer do you need to be an amateur to compete at the Olympics; the gold medals that were once a symbol of an amateur sporting ethos and a dedication to excellence are reduced to being bargaining chips for professional athletes and dream teams as they seek to negotiate another multimillion dollar sponsorship deal.

Looking at some of the sums involved, it's enough to make your eyes water. Just a tiny fraction of the annual salary of an international soccer player or an NBA star would be enough to keep our little club going for years, and as we scrabble around for the pennies we need to start a youth project and try to bring the game to a new generation of non-Irish players, I often think the easiest way to find it might be to pick up the phone to Wayne Rooney and ask him for a cheque. With a name like that and a wife called Colleen, he's bound to have some Irish ancestry. Whatever about the ancestry, he could definitely afford it.

When we started out we had a very simple idea to get sponsorship: five sponsors, €500 each, parity across the board. No matter what business they were in — be it pubs or pharmaceuticals, travel or entertainment — we would try to find some way of including them and their customers in what we did. In hindsight this was nowhere near enough, but as we were an unknown quantity it was about the maximum I thought we could get. Having looked at the cost of renting halls and subsidising tournament registration fees with a few quid, this seemed about right.

Added to this €2,500 was a development grant from the GAA. Brilliant, I thought, as county secretary Tony Bass asked me for our bank details so he could arrange the transfer of the money. A few thousand euro would go a long way towards helping us establish ourselves, getting in with the city and maybe finding a bit of ground where we could have our own pitch. All those ideas stopped when the grant arrived. Three hundred euro was enough to buy six footballs, if we got O'Neills to knock a few quid off because we were buying in bulk.

Convinced there was more money to be had I started to dig around, but it wasn't long before I found myself in the twilight zone that is government policy and GAA politics. It wasn't simply a case of going to the local embassy and asking for a hand-out. The government makes money available through various schemes and ministries, which is then distributed by the GAA.

There are other funds available, but they are not the kind of people who advertise in *The Irish Times* and say 'come and get me'. In order to get your hands on this money, you have to know it exists, and even that is not enough. You also have to know how to ask for it. As well as being European County Board secretary, Tony Bass is a master of the political arena, having worked as an adviser to the Irish government and several EU presidencies. He does a great job networking and finding out what is available. But given the vast array of different funds available and the specific application processes for each one, it's almost a full-time job just keeping abreast of it all.

Even if the embassies themselves can't help directly when it comes to financing, they are still a great resource and not just somewhere to go when you need a new passport. The Irish ambassador to Stockholm, Donal Hamill, has been tremendously supportive of the Stockholm Gaels in our first year, and his second secretary Ragnar Almqvist is an active member of the club. I'd sincerely doubt the ambassador took this into account when appointing him, but Ragnar is a tremendous Gaelic footballer and a former goalkeeper for the Kilmacud Crokes club. Son of a Swedish academic and born and raised in Dublin, he's also a fluent Irish speaker, and with his background in the civil service, he is invaluable in helping us negotiate the murky waters of state support.

The embassy also helps keep us in touch with the rest of the Irish community. Strange as it may seem, there are people who don't have a whole lot of interest in sport, and indeed there are Irish people who don't have a great need or desire to socialise with other Irish people. Either way it's good to know what and who is out there and to at least offer them the chance to be involved if they so wish.

The situation with government funding is not unique, and as clubs we tend to make a few fundamental mistakes in our assumptions when we go looking for money. The area of corporate sponsorship is not as simple as it might look, and even though there are a few businesses that are flush with cash, very few of them are inclined to give it away just for the fun of it.

Ireland's ambassador to Denmark, Brendan Scannell, tells a wonderful story about asking a hotel owner in Japan if he wouldn't mind contributing a few quid to the running of the club. The hotel owner thought for a moment. As a Japanese businessman he wasn't exactly from hurling stock, but given that this was a personal request he took it seriously. 'How much does it cost to run the club for the year?' he asked. Scannell, a great GAA fan who had joined the foreign service the same day as Donal Hamill and had served his country abroad for over 30 years, thought for a moment. 'I'd say it costs about €20,000, give or take, so any contribution would be most welcome,' said the diplomat. 'OK,' said the hotel owner, who subsequently sent a cheque for €20,000 to the club. Even if it wasn't the ambassador's intention that the hotelier should contribute the full amount for the year, I doubt if any money was ever sent back to him with a polite note saying, thanks, but no thanks.

The ambassador's success in Japan is very much a once-off and even with the help of the country's diplomatic corps, sponsorship money can be very hard to come by. The major mistake that most clubs make is that we think primarily of what's in it for us, rather than what's in it for the sponsor. Businessmen didn't get where they are by firing money into a massive hole for no return, so that tactic isn't going to get us very far. We need to offer them something concrete. What kind of exposure can we offer them? Do they get a thousand hits a day on our website? Is there a customer base they can tap into? If we want to make the GAA a viable, long-term proposition, then the old days of just having the pub logo on the shirt have surely passed.

Then there is the budgeting process itself. Even if pitches and balls and kit cost a few quid, they pale into insignificance when compared to what the players themselves contribute. However much they love to play the game, there is a limit to what an individual can afford to invest in what is essentially a hobby. It might mean the world to us but it is a hobby just the same. Given that our club was new on the scene and that we had little or no experience of how to organise tournaments, we didn't host a round of the Scandinavian championship in Stockholm, which left us with four lengthy away trips to some of the most expensive countries in the world in which to drink beer. On average we had to take a couple of hours off on a Friday to drive around 500 kilometres to the host city in a hired minibus. About €60 will pay for your place on the bus plus the diesel required to get you there. Even if we stayed in hostels, a bed for the night will still set you back €20 or €30. The match registration fee of €35 usually covers lunch and dinner for each player on the day of the tournament, but there's always a lunch or a dinner or a bag of bananas that needs to be bought on the way there or back. So before a champagne cork is popped or a pint ordered, attending a tournament costs about €200, plus whatever couple of hours is lost at work. It wouldn't be unreasonable for many of the lads to spend €50 at the post-tournament party. As all four tournaments this season were away from home, that's €1,000 each man has to pay to take part, on top of the €50 annual membership fee we charge. Most of this expense is concentrated during a few short months during the summer. With families expecting to be brought on holidays, it can be a heavy burden to bear.

The financial future of clubs in Europe and further afield is dependent on three factors. The first of these is in packaging their activities to attract corporate sponsors either from local Irish-owned businesses or from outside the Irish community, with the obvious goal being that every club finds its own benevolent Japanese hotelier to be their Abramovic.

The second is to get themselves well enough organised to take a bigger share of the government funding that is available, both from Ireland and their host country. No country may be as completely consumed by sport as Ireland, but the Scandinavian countries in particular invest huge amounts of money in sporting organisations and facilities, as do the EU. Municipalities in Sweden have massive budgets for sport, and if our clubs can get just a tiny fraction of this, it would make a vast difference. Clubs that have their house in order financially and learn how these and other application and grants processes work will find themselves benefiting enormously from resources that other organisations take for granted.

The third is perhaps the most unfortunate, even if it is a silver lining for many clubs outside Ireland. The mass exodus from Ireland caused by the appalling mismanagement of the economy is already being reflected in the memberships of the clubs around Europe and further afield. Universities in Europe are filling up with Irish students looking for economical ways to complete their education, and our club has seen a massive upswing in the numbers turning up for training. In August in particular we had an influx of young players, male and female, who felt that studying abroad for a year or two represented their best chance of surviving the crisis. However temporary these new members may be, we are delighted to have them. There is also an influx of Irish people who can no longer stand firm against the tide; their Swedish partners want to move to Sweden, and with little or no prospects of jobs or a better future, it's hard to argue against it.

The membership fees paid by these people who in better times would have spent their careers back home are swelling the coffers of foreign-based clubs, and even if they don't become full-time, permanent playing members, they have their uses. With a dozen or more students available at training, it's much easier to replicate game situations, and the refugees from hurling counties like Limerick, Kilkenny and Tipperary are often delighted to get the chance to show off their skills, skills that are otherwise in short supply outside of Ireland.

Chapter 12 ⌒
| ANY GIVEN SATURDAY

Outside the window the Swedish countryside flashes by in a late-summer blur of greens and browns and golds. The rhythmic clack of the train on the track this sunny Friday afternoon has already lulled most of those that share my carriage to sleep, but not me. My stomach churns anxiously; these are not the butterflies associated with nerves before a big event. Nor is it blind, inexplicable panic. I know exactly what I have to do.

Instead, it feels like a swarm of angry wasps, fuelled by dry sandwiches and bitter coffee, buzzing away inside and threatening to consume me. Tomorrow we take the field in the final round of the Scandinavian Gaelic Football Championship and in my whole life I have never been this close to winning anything. The thought that we could somehow slip up and blow it is eating me up inside. We started in the spring with nothing, and we have come too far, trained and worked and fought too hard to fall at the final hurdle. Too many have sacrificed too much. It cannot be allowed to happen. I cannot allow it to happen.

This time I've travelled on my own to the final tournament of the year, and as the train pulls into the station, I pull my cramped and stiff body up out of my seat, stretching myself out as I go. Kit bag slung over my shoulder, I step off the train into the afternoon sun and head off to the hostel, the swarm of wasps buzzing so loudly in my gut that I expect passers-by to hear them.

The train is a great way to travel, but immediately when I arrive I regret having done so on my own. The journey on the minibus is long and arduous but made all the shorter by the craic in the back. There is plenty of time for talking about previous matches and games to come and to gossip about opponents. It is on these long journeys that the boys and girls who wear the black of the Stockholm Gaels have got to know each other. And as I trudge up the platform at the Nils Ericsson station in Gothenburg, I feel like nothing without my team.

It's a short bus ride to the hostel on the outskirts of Sweden's second city, but I get off a stop early just for the exercise. I have plenty of time to spare. After an interminable wait the lads start to arrive. Those that flew down are in first and as the easy laughter starts to flow, the buzzing of the wasps starts to subside. Then the car and the minibus, both crammed to bursting point with people and the usual cargo of kit, video cameras, balls, water bottles, magazines and iPods. For once they didn't have to put up with Seán Beatty on a sugar buzz on the bus as he's working back in Stockholm. As soon as he has finished his shift in the Dubliner, he'll head to the bus station and travel all night to get here, arriving at about six in the morning.

The girls split and go searching for their room; even though their game tomorrow is only an exhibition, they approach it as if it was an All-Ireland final in Croke Park. For Maja and Malin it's their first competitive game, and Maja seems more nervous than the rest of us put together. As the door closes behind them, the humour level drops another couple of notches, and the wasps are quiet for the first time in a long time.

By the time they arrive the restaurant has closed, so Keith and a few of the lads go off in search of food, returning soon with bags full of the food of champions — Big Macs and fries. Phil Cahill pulls up a high stool at the bar. As our coach he won't be playing and is exempt from the booze ban that is in place the night before every tournament. He takes it upon himself to police the booze ban, and with his reputation as a footballer and his broad shoulders, it would be a brave man that tried to deceive him. Goalkeeper Liam is allowed to join him for a beer as he hopefully won't have too much running to do tomorrow, but the lads aren't interested in drinking anyway. As everyone arrives in the lobby, our attention is already turning to tomorrow.

Niall talks in his soft northern burr about how we are going to approach the day. We've beaten all these teams before — in some cases, hammered them — but Gaelic football is not the kind of game where merely showing up is enough to claim the spoils. He reminds us that the lads on the other teams are every bit as proud of their clubs as we are of ours, and that they will be going out to take us down a peg or two if they can. We slaughtered Gothenburg in our first-ever game, and now that we are coming to their home ground, they're going to be looking to pay us back. Revenge is a great motivator, and we'll have to be on our guard if we are not to slip up. With Niall's words ringing in our ears, we turn in for the night.

I'd love to be able to claim that I slept like a baby, sure of my role in the team and certain we would win, but I don't. I read and I surf the internet and try to relax, but when I turn out the light and close my eyes the images from tomorrow are already in front of me, an old habit from reading too many sports psychology books.

We are on the pitch in our black jerseys, focused, tense, ready for action. The ref throws the ball up and Deccy breaks it down to Colin. A quick hand pass to Niall, who strides purposefully through the middle and lays it off to Ken and screams for the return, which duly comes. He knows he has them now, and every stride pulls them more out of shape. Desperate decisions are made. The defence begins to collapse in on top of him, but he moves fluidly, drawing them in and then shrugging off the tackles. Two defenders descend on him now, intent on putting a stop to his gallop by fair means or foul. He prepares himself for the inevitable pain as he bears down on goal, and then at the last second before impact he loops a fisted pass to his left over the onrushing defenders to me.

The two defenders smash into him, sending all three sprawling in a tangle of arms and legs. The referee sees that I've caught the ball and waves play on. Realising he's not going to get anything, Niall rises to his knees and watches the play unfold.

I'm gloriously free, with only the goalkeeper to beat. I take a bounce, look up and see the fear in his eyes. He makes up his mind and starts his kamikaze rush out of the goal to close me down, narrowing the angle. I could wait for him to make it out to me, drop the shoulder and go round him, but I'm not in the mood for waiting. Calmly, I drop the ball to strike it with my right foot . . . I wake with a jolt as the ball leaves my boot, enveloped in the silent darkness of a Gothenburg hostel. It's going to be a long night.

It feels like I've only closed my eyes when the long night is cut short by Seán calling me on the phone. It's six o'clock in the morning and he has arrived in Gothenburg and there is not a soul on the streets. He takes a taxi to our hostel on the outskirts of town and I let him into our little room where we chat for a few minutes before he passes out, desperate to grab a bit of rest before the long day's march towards the championship begins.

Even though I only met him at the St Patrick's Day celebrations a couple of years ago, it feels like I've known him forever. We started playing soccer together soon after we met, and after years of playing with Swedes who barely say a word on the pitch, it was fantastic to have someone beside me on the field who never stopped talking. The fact that he's also a northside Dub helps and we quickly formed a partnership up front that brought goal after goal and saw us rise to the top of the table. The productive partnership only faltered when I poked home a shot from Seán that was going over the line anyway. He was incensed at me for stealing his goal, and after that there were no more passes from Seán to run on to as we both played for ourselves for a while, both vying to be the team's top scorer. Eventually the toe-poke was forgotten about and I vowed never to do it again. Hell hath no fury like a Cabra man robbed of a goal.

I can't get back to sleep and soon I'm in the shower getting ready for the day ahead. Given the lack of sleep I'm exhausted before we even begin, and I wonder how many players have spent sleepless nights before taking the field at Lansdowne Road or Croke Park. For many of us in this team, this is about as big as it's ever going to get. This is our All-Ireland final.

It doesn't surprise me that Billy and the lads have a great facility to host a football tournament. As one of the oldest clubs in the region — formed way back in 2004 — they have a head start over the rest of us, and they now share a ground with a rugby club, complete with dressing rooms, showers and even a clubhouse with a little bar and the Irish sports channels. The pitch is in good nick apart from a few patches of lying water that should hopefully dry up during the day. I make up my mind not to take a bounce near the goal at one end; the ball could die with a splat in a muddy puddle and leave me looking very stupid indeed.

Whether or not I'll get the chance is open to question. Starting my own business has taken its toll time-wise and aside from missing the Oslo tournament, I haven't made a single Wednesday night session at Gärdet since before the summer began. Gärdet is where Phil Cahill does the hard work, building up conditioning and drilling the skills into the team, and I haven't been there. It doesn't matter that I've been training every day by myself or that I've kicked hundreds of points in preparation. All this counts for nothing. Phil is unlikely to play me sight unseen.

The conversation at the bar with Phil last night threw up another issue. His tactical approach to the game is very different to Niall's. Whereas our original coach from Antrim favoured the short-passing possession game so beloved of teams from the North, Phil's style is much more pragmatic. Colin Courtney is the fastest forward in Scandinavia, so no matter where or when you get the ball on the pitch, you hit him with it. Phil wants the ball up the field quickly and the ball over the bar or in the back of the net with the minimum amount of fuss or bother.

Whereas Niall's style of play was designed to keep the ball out of the hands of the opposition, Phil seems to see it differently. For him, every short pass is a risk, especially in your own half. Better to hit the ball long up the field and if there is any short passing to be done, do it in front of the opponent's goal instead of messing around in front of your own.

Given the fact that I have all the speed and mobility of Nelson's Pillar, I have a feeling this is going to limit my contribution. If Colin is going to be more or less a lone forward and the fulcrum of the attack, then I'm not sure how I or any other forward is going to fit into the picture. Robbed of the tactical certainty I enjoyed in Malmö when I played instead of Ciarán at midfield, doubts creep in.

Captain Carroll comes into the dressing room. 'It's probably not the draw ye wanted lads, but it's Malmö up first again.' I look around at the rest of the lads and I'm not sure I agree. We all know that to be sure of winning the championship, we will need to beat every team here today at least once. The order in which we do that is immaterial.

As we've never staged a tournament ourselves I'm not really sure how the whole draw system works, but it seems the host clubs like to take us on as early as possible in the day. When playing so many games in one day, the timetable has to have rest periods built in for each team and these must be distributed as fairly as possible. But in three of the four tournaments so far we have faced the hosts in our first game, with Copenhagen being the only one to buck the trend. The schedule showed we were due to face Gothenburg in the opener, but a couple of minutes later it was torn down and redrawn.

Less than 24 hours before the tournament was due to begin, Oslo pulled out. With the possible exception of their own, every tournament was touch and go for the Norwegians as they struggled to get the numbers necessary to field a team. Their results on the field didn't help either, even if they didn't really reflect the standard of their play. It's hard to get people to play regularly, let alone spend money travelling to tournaments, when you're getting beaten in virtually every game. This was for them a sad state of affairs because in actual fact Oslo were a tough side to meet and scores were only piled up against them towards the end of games as they tired and lacked fresh legs.

So for the third time in four tournaments we would open against our old foes from Malmö, and it was impossible to know what to expect. Would the physically dominant side that showed up in Copenhagen take the field, or would it be the yo-yo outfit that made the trips to Gothenburg and Oslo? The answer was a little bit of both.

'Niall! Niall! Kevin! Kick it in! Kick it in!' barks Phil from the touchline. It's a simple enough tactic, so why are we having such a hard time grasping it? Phil has left me on the sideline, favouring Keith for the right half forward position he wants to fill, but I'm not too bothered to begin with. It's going to be a long day and besides, I prefer to start out somewhere on the left so I can cut inside and shoot off my right foot.

But it's messy. As soon as they win the ball in defence, our lads are instinctively looking for a short pass to start working the ball up the field. Phil roars his disapproval from the sideline as Niall dallies on the ball. The tactic is not just to hit it long, but to hit it early and give Colin the chance to use his speed to beat his man to the ball and turn with it. But Niall is almost too intelligent a footballer for that. Rather than hitting just any old long ball, he wants to hit a good one for Colin to run on to. But Phil is not prepared to wait.

The sun is breaking through the clouds now and not before time. Heavy rain had fallen the whole week leading up to the tournament and it has taken its toll on the playing surface. It was badly in need of some warmth to dry it out. The surface cuts up underfoot, not least when Colin goes to make his sharp turns with the ball. The muck flies up as his studs lose their grip in the turf, planting him face first in the dirt. When he does manage to keep his feet, there are Malmö defenders to contend with, and they don't seem to have anything against climbing up his back to stop him from turning to face the goal. They are careful not to give away too much close to their own goal, but as soon as he starts to approach the halfway line they climb aboard and don't disembark until the referee's whistle blows. Not a pretty tactic but annoyingly it's very effective, and in fairness if I was facing Courtney in full flight I'd probably do a whole lot worse.

The physical stuff is on both sides, with both teams wasting long kick-outs by conceding cheap frees to the defending team. The ball is kicked back and forth with neither team getting it into any dangerous positions.

Malmö face the same problems as we do in their attack. They too are blessed with some very intelligent footballers, and they seek to draw our defenders towards the middle of the pitch before dinking the ball in behind our corner backs. On a better surface they would no doubt have racked up appreciably more scores. But the slipping and sliding and the dead surface take their toll, and the few gilt-edged chances that do appear are snatched wide. Referee Martin O'Connell hasn't had to make many ticks in his notebook during the first half, with both sides only managing to register a point each.

At the half-time whistle Phil repeats the mantra. 'Lads, don't be hanging around. We've got the fastest, best forward in Scandinavia up there, and I don't want him standing looking at you fellas playing football. I want him on the ball and scoring, so stop messing around and get the ball up to him.' Kevin and Niall back him up, and we're off again with me taking over from Keith in the half forward line.

The second half gets off to a flyer as Ken is rugby-tackled after the throw-in. Niall drops the ball in close to the Malmö goal, and from the resultant mêlée Colin is awarded a penalty. This is the first time Martin has refereed our team and it always takes time to get used to how they work and what they are likely to call, but in a game where we were finding it hard to get scores on the board, the new referee all of a sudden found himself in sympathy with us on this occasion.

Colin stroked home the penalty and we lifted our game a notch, but still we couldn't find our range. Colin got free down the left only for the ball to balloon off his boot as he went to finish, and as Declan slashed through the middle he missed a chance he'd normally knock over with his eyes closed. Kevin Carroll showed his worth as captain, coaxing instead of criticising us, and when he had a chance himself a minute later he clipped it over cleanly, oblivious to the pressure and the misses that had gone before.

Off out on the right along the sodden sideline, I'm foraging around looking for a bit of space and a bit of dry ground to work in. Malmö are packing their defence and staying put, so contrary to Phil's wishes we have to pass the ball a lot more as we probe for an opening, and we're getting good results down our side.

Suddenly Niall is bursting through the middle again; about to get swallowed up, he pops the ball to me and I drill it over the bar. We're five points ahead now and aside from one scramble from a free kick, Malmö have barely threatened us at all. Carroll fires over another and coach Cahill goes to the bench. It's time to close out the game.

But before we do, one more chance falls to me. Drifting out on the right again, I find myself through on goal. I've been over this situation a thousand times and the only thought in my mind is to bury this ball and this match once and for all and try to book my place in the team to start the next one. The rest of the lads have had their chances to impress Phil over the previous weeks at Gärdet. This was mine.

With the goal at my mercy, I'm going to play it safe. This close in, there is little chance of hitting it wide, but being six points ahead there are still only two goals in the difference. Seeing as they had barely created a chance in the second half, the thought that Malmö would somehow conjure up two goals in the dying minutes seemed ridiculous, but I was undeterred. This ball was either going over the bar, or under the bar. One way or another I was going to score.

At the very last second I aimed high into the centre of the goal and smashed the ball as hard as I could. If it went too high, it would still go over and I would have put us seven points ahead and well out of sight. A foot lower and the goalkeeper would have no chance to get both hands over his head quick enough to stop it, and I would have bagged my third goal in three group games against Malmö.

The ball crashes off the crossbar and bounces down a yard over the line before spinning back out. I look at the umpire. He shakes his head. No goal. Play on. Crushed.

I had laughed along with everyone else when Frank Lampard had a goal disallowed for England against Germany at the World

Cup, despite the fact that it was miles over the line. I wasn't laughing now. A minute later the final whistle sounded. We'd won, but we'd made heavy weather of it.

Copenhagen were up next in a game that showed why the biggest health difficulty associated with sport is not some physical injury, but a kind of sporting schizophrenia. Nothing else could explain how the teams contesting this championship could swing from one extreme to the other in the course of a season, a tournament, or even a game.

That Phil kept me in the team felt like a vindication of sorts. Despite the merciless slagging administered for the disallowed goal, I'd done OK against Malmö. I hadn't given the ball away and I had taken my point well when I had the chance. There had obviously been some consultation between Niall and Phil and following the decent performance against the Danes at the Gothenburg tournament, and I would once again be patrolling the midfield against them.

This game would be make or break; win here and the road to the final — and the championship title — was a lot easier to negotiate. Lose and we'd have little time to lick our wounds before taking on the hosts, whom we would probably need to beat if we were to progress.

As we lined out and waited for the ball to be thrown in, I thought back to the very first day of the championship when we'd looked on as Copenhagen and Malmö played the first Scandinavian championship match that any of us had ever seen. I was taken aback by the tough play, the occasionally nasty fouls and the breakneck tempo of the game, and to be honest I wouldn't have fancied meeting either of them. A couple of short months later I was lining out against them in midfield, comfortable in the knowledge that we had beaten them every time we had faced them, and that probably the best game I had played all season had been against a team that I had originally feared.

Copenhagen, for their part, had never seemed the same after the first round. They were the oldest club in the region and the reigning champions in the European Shield, but despite their obvious ability they hadn't even made it to the final of their own tournament. They went through the motions against us in Gothenburg and with their championship aspirations for the year down the tubes, they hadn't been able to get enough players to go to Oslo. A lot of teams might not have bothered showing up for the last regional round in those circumstances, but all credit to them for doing so.

Whatever about giving them credit, Courtney wasn't in a generous mood as he netted an early goal, and when Dec slammed over a point from miles out the field it looked like we were going to run away with it. Beatty seemed to have taken on the role of playmaker, passing to Colin for his opening goal before setting Jim Kelly free. With one of the only shots he took all season, the Longford man landed a left-footer that would be among the candidates for the best of the year.

I was doing my best in midfield, but other than linking up the play my major contribution was to drag down Copenhagen's John Lambert, giving him an easy free to put them on the board. A superbly skilful player, Lambert had been taking the long route to goal, heading towards the sideline before turning back in, ghosting past defender after defender, none of whom could stop him. I took a short cut from my midfield position and straight through our half back line, where I brought him to a halt with a challenge more commonly seen in the World Wrestling Federation. Free in. I was lucky not to get booked.

Phil Cahill wasn't impressed. A teak-tough defender himself, there were two things he didn't care for: high tackles and giving away kickable frees. I had just done both. 'Put it right, Phil,' he growled from the sideline. I took it as a direct order rather than a suggestion.

I wouldn't have long to wait. Kevin Carroll was back hunting around our half back line. Out of a forest of legs, he came up with the ball and fired it off into the corner for me to chase. I wasn't sure I'd make it before the ball went out of play, but I knew Phil had his eye on me, and if I didn't chase it down it wouldn't be long before I'd be joining him on the bench and Keith would be back in. I pin my ears back and race the ball to the touchline, where I barely manage to keep it in play.

I don't have to bother beating the first defender; he has turned around to tell the referee the ball was out and demand the ball back, so I fly past him as he protests. No dice. Play on. I may not be the fastest player in the world, but once I get into my stride and build up a head of steam I can be hard to stop. I keep going, looking to pass the ball into the middle, but I'm going too quickly now to take it all in. I change direction, wrong-footing another defender, and the posts open up in front of me. I lift the ball gently over the bar to put another precious point between us. I give Kevin the thumbs-up for the pass that set me free and in return I get credit for chasing down a lost cause and turning it into a score. The confidence level rises. I might just deserve to be here after all.

Beatty is at it again, sliding a ball through for Colin to net his second goal, and we're motoring now. We're still not hitting the scores as fluently as we should and a few balls are still dropping harmlessly into the goalkeeper's arms, but we're unrecognisable from the team that faced Malmö. Scullion rounds off the period with a point, and we finish the first half with a comfortable lead. Another goal in the second half puts an end to the Danish challenge for this year. We have one foot in the final, and after 15 games and just a single defeat, the Scandinavian championship is within our grasp.

———

'Lads, what the fuck was that?' Whatever your chosen sport, it's never a positive sign when the half-time team talk starts with these words. Phil isn't angry or annoyed or pissed off. He's baffled by what he has just seen. Regardless of the black jerseys with the crest on them, the football played in the first half of the first game of the final tournament doesn't resemble any Stockholm team any of us have ever seen before.

What Phil had just seen from the sideline was probably the worst game of Gaelic football any of us ever saw, at any level. I don't know if being the home team means they are distracted or feeling the pressure more than usual. For us it's very simple: win this game and we can't be caught. We've won the Scandinavian championship at the first time of asking. All we had to do was continue the amazing unbeaten run that started when we took our revenge on Malmö. As it stood, Gothenburg needed to shut us down. They could afford to lose the game, but if the margin was more than four points it would be Malmö who would face us in the final and have one last shot at stopping the Stockholm juggernaut that had rolled around Scandinavia for most of the summer.

It's not happening. Footballers who have played to the highest standards in some thrilling encounters throughout the season now can't kick a simple pass or tap a ball over the bar from a few yards out, and that goes for both sides. It could be described as being comically bad, but for the two teams looking to get to the final, there was nothing funny about it.

Gothenburg are a tough nut to crack at the best of times with Billy marshalling the defence, and they don't lack firepower up front either. Keith Creamer's fluid football skills make him dangerous from anywhere on the pitch, and as if keeping an eye on him wasn't enough, you had the likes of the wily Declan Redmond and Niall O'Connor to deal with. But with the ball kicked back and forth and neither side able to control it for any meaningful period of time, there were no decent chances to speak of. The free-scoring friendly in Stockholm back in August was a dim and distant memory as both teams struggled to create something, and the game limped towards half-time with Stockholm leading by the slimmest of margins. The football was so bad even the sun wouldn't watch it and it snuck in behind the safety of the clouds to wait for the final whistle.

'Lads, take a feckin' pop. Stop messin' around. We have lads out there who can shoot, so do it. Niall can do it. Declan can do it. Colin, you can do it. Phil can do it. Just set yourself and shoot.'

I was surprised to hear my name mentioned but delighted to hear Phil say I could shoot. I was pretty hard on myself when it came to converting chances and I was still smarting from the disallowed goal against Malmö which would have made the win much more comprehensive. Unreasonable as it may sound, I expect myself to score every time I shoot, and anything else is just giving the ball away. So it meant a lot to hear something like that from Phil Cahill, a fella who was no slouch as a player himself. All thoughts of the ball smacking off the crossbar against Malmö disappeared. If I had a chance in the second half I wasn't going to shirk the responsibility. I was going to go for it.

It didn't last long. We quickly fashioned a chance at the start of the second half and Declan found me free about 25 metres out. I steadied myself, swung my boot and watched as the ball drifted gently just to the right of the goal and wide. So much for Phil Cahill's faith in my shooting, I thought. Chances like that hadn't come along too often in the first period, and I'd blown the first opportunity in the second half.

But it was to be the first of many misses as the nerves spread through the team like a virus. No bookmaker in the world would have taken bets on Kevin Carroll not scoring as he bore down on goal, but he smacked his effort wide. Shortly after that it was

Declan's turn as a mishit effort flew harmlessly out over the end line for a goal kick.

Niall Scullion strode up from the back to put an end to the malaise, but dropped his kick short and into the arms of the goalkeeper. It was starting to get silly as chance after chance went a-begging, and to make matters worse, Keith Creamer went up the other end and scored to put Gothenburg level.

Back down at the Gothenburg goal, the torn-up pitch had Colin slipping and sliding all over the place as he tried to pull his marker away and create a half-chance. Having missed a relatively simple chance, I've given up shooting. Besides, I have my hands full trying to keep track of the deceptively quick Niall O'Connor, who is starting to give me the runaround. But if the misses bother the rest of the lads, it doesn't show. Scullion breaks up the field once again, and this time he pops one over. Three points to two for us. Kevin Carroll breaks free again, but even though he's running at full pace, when he belts the ball goalwards it too drops inexplicably short and into the welcoming arms of the goalkeeper.

Finally, all the slipping and sliding pays off as Courtney is brought down. He slots over the free kick himself to give us a two-point lead with just a couple of minutes to go. The chances of Gothenburg scoring a goal seem remote but you never can tell.

A scramble ensues about ten metres out from our goal and Gothenburg peg another point back. Our lead is cut to a single point. The last minute of the game goes on for an eternity. If we can hold on, we become champions of Scandinavia at the final whistle, despite this being easily the worst game we have ever played. But in years to come no one will remember that. Despite the fact that we'd love to secure the title scoring a half-dozen goals in a free-flowing display, winning ugly is still winning.

Finally, after a minute that seemed to last longer than all the games in the rest of the season put together, the whistle goes to put us all out of our misery. We've hung on. We are champions of Scandinavia at the first time of asking, and the shouts of joy are mixed with sighs of relief.

The day isn't over, and even though the final isn't as bad as the first half of the previous game — it couldn't be — it's still a turgid affair. The sun reappears and the heat adds to the fatigue. But this is a tournament final, and it has to be won.

'C'mon lads!' says Kevin Carroll, urging the boys on. 'It's like Al Pacino said in *Any Given Sunday*. This is a game of inches, so let's go out there and give it all we've got.' We have no idea what he's on about. Gaelic football has virtually nothing in common with American football. We put his odd team talk down to the fact that he's run out of things to say and has started worrying about what he's going to say when he has to make an acceptance speech later. So with these words from Carroll and Al Pacino, we head into the fray once more, tired but utterly determined that our near-perfect record won't be spoiled any further.

All the chasing of the previous game has taken its toll, and the two teams look lethargic. I've started on the half forward line. Phil wants us to clear out the middle of the field, and Liam has instructions to deliver his goal kicks out to the wings. But we're completely empty by now, and we lack the pace and power to get to Liam's kick-outs before they run harmlessly out of play. We seem to be doing a lot of running for nothing.

At so many different points during the season, players have stepped up when we needed them most, and in this final it is Declan Graham's turn. You never really know where you have big Dec. A quiet, unassuming giant of a man of few words, he's never happier than when he's on a football pitch, or better still a hurling one — that or possibly snoozing. His love of sleep is legendary, and as a team we're very thankful for it, because whatever energy he conserves seems to be kept for when he's on the pitch.

His natural ability means he can play in any position on the field, and in the final he is in at full forward again. The positional switches don't seem to bother him, and he seems to know what to do with the ball instinctively, no matter where he's playing. With our precious unbeaten record under threat, Declan calmly slots a goal either side of half-time before dropping further out the pitch. It's in marked contrast to my own contribution; lost and drifting badly at half forward, Phil takes me off before half-time, much to my frustration.

It's not much of a spectacle either for the spectators, one of whom Kevin Carroll clatters as he tackles his man out over the sideline. With about ten minutes left to go in the season, Kevin is still going at the same breakneck speed as when it started.

There is time for one more outrageously brilliant score from Colin Courtney. A poor pass from out on the right flies over his head and runs along the ground towards the goal line. Running out of space and with the angle narrowing all the time, he sizes up the situation quickly before banging the ball over the crossbar, wrapping his foot around the ball with a first-time shot off the ground. A couple of minutes later he nets his last goal of the season and Phil calls him ashore to give Barry Quinn a run. The job that started in May in Copenhagen is now complete.

The dressing room is loud with laughter as some of the lads get changed, ready to hit the town straight away. The bar of the rugby club does a brisk trade in the sunshine, and no one seems in a hurry to leave. It's as if by packing our bags and heading off we will be closing the door on the season, and none of us can be certain it will ever be this good again.

I feel sorry for the Malmö boys. An intense rivalry has built up between our two clubs and I'd sincerely doubt we've heard the last of it. But it can't have been easy for them to have us come along and knock them off their perch. Last year they were the new club sweeping all before them, and no doubt they had hoped that that situation would continue for the foreseeable future. But it wasn't to be, and despite the obvious differences in how we are as clubs and as individuals, I'm enjoying this chance to spend a few minutes talking to them. Secretly I think Ginge and I are already looking forward to next season. He wants revenge for this one, and I'm owed a goal by that damn umpire.

There is a festival in Gothenburg this weekend and people throng the streets as we make our way to the Dubliner, a sister pub of our Stockholm sponsor, for the last reception of the year. Ravenously hungry again, we enjoy the food and a few drinks before Billy gives out the prizes. I'm still wandering around with our video camera, trying to capture some of the fun with Niall O'Connor from Gothenburg giving me stick. He enjoyed giving me the runaround earlier in the day and sees no reason to stop now. The camera has been with us all through the journey and one of these days we'll edit the whole thing together into a little documentary about our first season. Like everything else, it's a matter of finding the time and the energy to do it.

Billy is making the presentations now — or at least he would be if the first one wasn't to himself for the poc fada. He won the Malmö one too, but seeing as he had two pucks and our own Liam Ginnane had only one, the trophy was 'liberated' from him at some point during the celebrations. He won fair and square today though.

Next up is the MVP, the player of the tournament as decided by the referees. Honourable mentions are given to players from all the teams, with Niall Scullion and Liam Ginnane from Stockholm getting a nod, and about the only one who is surprised when Kevin Carroll's name is called out as the MVP is Kevin himself.

Apart from the final team talk, he has been rock solid all day. Even after a couple of misses, his head never went down and he just motored on, picking off points when they were most needed and winning breaking ball all over the field. There might be others that have a tiny bit more skill, but more than any other player, Kevin is the heart of this team. We didn't lose a game all year when he played.

His speech is another improvised beauty too. Roundly heckled to begin with, he thanks the lads from Gothenburg and our two sponsors who are in attendance, Niall Balfe and Liam Kennedy, and to finish he recalls a conversation he had with Malmö's Mark Rattigan after the final. 'I was having this chat with Mark back at the rugby club, and we were discussing the Irish in Sweden and all that craic, and how easy it is for the single lads to settle, and how much harder it is for us that are married. But you see this, lads? You see this here? This means everything, and long may it continue.' Even the hardest of the hard men melt a little inside. Kevin is handed his prize, then the trophy for winning the Gothenburg round, and the collection is almost complete. Next season we'll add the Copenhagen trophy that we're missing.

Being from Limerick, Billy possesses a bizarre sense of humour, and the Gothenburg players have organised a 'Blind Date' competition as part of the evening's entertainment. Declan and Maja, who made a brilliant impression along with Malin Leander as both made their debuts for the ladies' team today, are our candidates. Declan's soft-spoken nature and his Antrim accent cause no end of hilarity, and Maja acquits herself well, even if she was hugely nervous. A guitar is produced and Niall belts out 'The Fields of Athenry' before handing it to me. I sit myself on a bar stool in the middle of about 60 Gaelic footballers and belt out 'Molly Malone' as loud as I can, and as I finish I can't resist one last dig.

'That's how it's done, culchies! That's how it's done!'

———

There's another parking ticket on the windscreen of the minibus when I get back to it, and I resign myself to the fact that it doesn't matter how long I live here, I will never understand the parking signs.

On the way we'd stopped by Keith Creamer's new pub, which is due to open the following Monday. Keith is not bothering to open an Irish pub, preferring instead to focus on food and jazz, and we wish him luck with it and promise to send whatever guests we can his way.

Back at the hostel I'm packing my bags before I even get into bed. Tomorrow morning I've an early train back to Stockholm to take Ingrid to her football practice. One of the conditions of being allowed to travel was that I would be back in time for that.

The relief is palpable. I honestly don't know what I would have done if we hadn't won here today. Maybe it would have been like losing the final in Copenhagen and spurred us on to even greater feats, but I doubt it. I wouldn't have been the only one to have considered packing it in if we had lost. As it was, I had played so badly in the final that it might be best for everyone if I did. But those thoughts won't last long, and with a bit of distance the memory of a poor performance in the final will retreat and we'll be left to look back on a season beyond our wildest dreams.

I awake again at six in the morning to find Beatty snoring in the next bed. Thoughtful lad that he is, he brought me home a cheeseburger in case I might need something for my breakfast in the morning, and placed it carefully on top of my folded-up jeans at the end of the bed. Throughout the hostel our team mates are scattered in various states of sobriety, and it strikes me that this is why I did it. This is why we all went through all the hassle, the training, the pain and the sleepless nights before tournaments. This is why I asked my family to make sacrifices, financial and otherwise, so that we could see it through to the end. Seán's little act of generosity is a symbol of what we are all looking for from this club — to know that someone is there for us.

Quietly I make my way out of the room and off towards the

bus stop. Waiting for the bus, it occurs to me that this is the first morning I woke up as a Scandinavian champion, and it feels good.

Up in Stockholm a little girl is asleep in her bed, and later on this afternoon she'll be taking the first steps in her sporting career. I intend to be there. Every step of the way.

Chapter 13

TÁ AN-ÁTHAS ORM AN CORN SEO A GHLACADH

I'm almost at the end of the list, and not before time. My shirt is stuck to my back; trying to conduct a prize-giving ceremony two weeks after being hospitalised with pneumonia is not something I'd recommend. There are no microphones in the large reception room at the new Irish Embassy in Stockholm, so the shallow breaths I manage to pull into my lungs have to carry all the way to the back of the room. Beads of sweat are forming on my forehead as we make our way towards the last presentation of the day, but I wouldn't have missed this for the world, even though the hardest part is yet to come.

The ambassador and his wife welcomed us all at the entrance to the magnificent new chancery. The lease was no doubt signed when Ireland knew more prosperous times, with beautiful views out over the water to the Stockholm archipelago beyond.

Jim Kelly has arrived before everyone else. I'm not sure how he got the job, but he seems to be the bartender for the evening, pouring perfect pints of stout and filling glasses of wine with his usual *bonhomie* as the catering staff go around with canapés. This will be the first official function at the new embassy, and it feels fitting that it is not for ministers or dignitaries but for ordinary Irish people.

Our season had not ended with the victory in Gothenburg, and over the following Sundays we had arranged a seven-a-side league to introduce new players and give everyone plenty of game time. Called the Ambassador Cup in recognition of the great support we had received from Ambassador Hamill and Ragnar, it was a highly competitive affair and the prizes were due to be handed out at this reception on the last Saturday in October. The ceremony was preceded by the first game of hurling in Stockholm in almost 15 years, and though I swore I wouldn't play due to the pneumonia, I couldn't help myself.

With one of the teams a man short and my wife a safe distance away in Barcelona, I rooted through the sports bags piled high on the sideline and fished out a pair of tracksuit bottoms and a jersey. No sooner had I gone on to the pitch at the start of the second half than a ball flashed across the goal. I pulled on it as hard as I could and it flew past Liam Ginnane and into the net. One touch, one goal, and that against a former Clare minor goalkeeper too. Not bad, I thought, for a Dub.

The sidelines weren't as full as they had been for the friendly against Gothenburg as the autumn chill kept people indoors, but there was still a good few spectators on hand to witness the game. Many of those had taken part in the Ambassador Cup and would be following us to the embassy to collect their winners' medals. The ambassador, allowing his name to be used, gave us the kind of credibility we couldn't buy otherwise, and we attracted a far broader range of players than previously.

First up were the new crop of students like Brendan O'Driscoll. Brendan's generation is totally different from mine. Born into the internet age and ready to travel, they know how to get things done. He came to Scandinavia to do a master's degree and as soon as he was accepted into the Royal School of Technology in Stockholm, he immediately set about contacting people here via the internet. He got in touch with us via the club website and we were able to help him find an apartment; in return we got a loyal and energetic player for five months who wholeheartedly supported everything the club did. Another man from a rugby background, he took to Gaelic football like a duck to water and in a few short weeks found himself challenging for his first medal with the Kennedy seven-a-side team. Unfortunately for him a final-day loss means he'll have to wait a little longer before he starts to fill the GAA shelf of his trophy cabinet. As he moves on to continue his studies in Gothenburg, Billy and the lads there will have the benefit of this bright, energetic young man and hopefully a few more like him when next season starts. But for all that, we're not going to do him any favours when we meet him on the pitch now that he's sleeping with the enemy.

Then there is the foreign contingent who took to the games, best personified by Guo Guodong. From China, Guo played soccer for Medborgarplatsen with Mark, Colin and Ken and was coaxed to come along and try out Gaelic football as we searched for players to take part in the Ambassador Cup.

If we were to find new players we had to stretch ourselves, so we aimed for four teams with at least seven players in each. That would mean we would need 28 players turning out every week for six weeks, even more if we wanted substitutes. Guo came down and learned the basic skills and rules of the game, and being a talented sportsman picking them up was no problem to him. Even so, few expected that a week later he would break away to score the winning goal in a hotly contested derby match between our two pub sponsors with the last kick of the game. An outstanding and unorthodox footballer, he will no doubt be knocking on the door of the championship squad next year.

Aside from the two pubs, the other two teams also came from our sponsors, Liam Kennedy's engineering firm Kennedy AB and Niall Balfe. It was fitting that it would be Niall's team that would win the cup for the first time. He had not just dug deep into his own pocket to support the club; he had turned up at every training session and done everything possible to smooth the club's path through its first year. He had even suffered a serious injury for the cause when he was slammed to the ground by Freddie in Oslo, and everyone in the club was delighted to see that he had recovered enough to lead his team on to the field in the final seven-a-side fixture. Despite the fragile shoulder, he led his squad to victory over Liam Kennedy's team, another man who had a lot in common with Niall when it came to supporting the club. Over the course of our first season Liam has been referee, emergency full forward, coach, sponsor and photographer, and he shows no signs of slowing down in his commitment. A medal from the ambassador was the very least these two deserved for their efforts.

The ambassador welcomes us all in Irish, Swedish and English. He speaks warmly about the club and the people he has met, and having seen more than one diplomat just going through the motions over the years, it's clear that this speech is completely genuine. We have agreed that he will make his remarks and then hand over to me. I will invite each of the recipients up one by one and the ambassador will present them with their medals.

Between the pneumonia, my wife being away and the hurling match, I hadn't even thought about my part in the day. I hadn't written a single word of what I wanted to say, but then again I didn't need to. We had spent the last six months together, living and breathing this club and chasing the championship, and I could talk about this team and these people for hours. I think the ambassador was probably afraid I would.

We started with the Ambassador Cup winners. Some of the players like Niall Balfe, Niall Scullion, Mark and Declan would be collecting two medals today, whereas Guo, Ericsson employee Mark Meagan and student Peter Conroy would have to content themselves with one — for this season at least.

Then it was the turn of the championship winners. When ordering the medals, a unanimous decision was taken that anyone who had played any part in any championship game would be eligible for a medal, as every single one of them had contributed to our remarkable series of victories in our first season.

As I introduced each player I took a moment to speak about them and what they brought to the club, starting with Barry Quinn. Being one of the few Dubs in the club and surrounded by strong characters from Meath and Kerry, not to mention the Antrim contingent bolstered by a hurling win over Dublin, I have given the lads a lot of stick throughout the season, with the 'c' word — culchie — being bandied about as much as possible. Try as I might, I couldn't think of a Carlow footballer to compare him to, and I said as much. The presentation ceremony wasn't just a chance for me to express my own gratitude for their commitment throughout the year; it was an opportunity to stand these guys up in front of their community and tell them about the contribution they had made. Like the medals they were to receive from the ambassador, this was the least they deserved.

I went on through the list, skipping my own name in the process, only to be hauled back by Kevin Carroll. For someone with no problem speaking or singing in front of others, I don't like the limelight when it is focused on me or what I have done. I didn't want this day to be about me or what we in the committee had done in setting up the club. This day was about honouring the players who had done so much to bring Gaelic games and a sense of pride to the city and the community, but Kevin stopped me as he collected his own medal to give a little speech giving me a lot of the credit. Whatever about not being prepared for the prize-giving, I certainly wasn't prepared for this, and for a few seconds I thought that the lump in my throat would stop me making it to the end of the list.

Through it all the trophy stood silent and shining on the table, and I still didn't know what I was going to say about it when the time came for it to be presented. How do you tell people that the

John Aherne trophy was named after a young man who had drowned on a visit to Stockholm two years previously? How do you explain the sense of helplessness we felt as an Irish community abroad as the days dragged on and John's body wasn't recovered from the icy waters? Or the sense of anger as the police called off their search as a bank holiday approached, leaving his family with a dreadful wait to find out his fate? How do you explain the burden carried since by the gregarious Karl Lambert, the Sundbyberg Express, with whom John was here to visit when he was so cruelly snatched from his friends and family? You don't. And I couldn't.

At that St Patrick's Day celebration in 2008, John was supposed to join us after the parade for a few drinks before heading back to Ireland on Monday. He'd left Karl and the lads in the pub the night before and headed off home to Karl's apartment where he was staying, and sometime after that he got to the apartment building where he went for a drink in the bar on the ground floor. He left the bar without his jacket, keys and mobile phone and was never seen alive again.

As the celebrations continued the following day, a worried Karl arrived at the post-parade party, but we waved away his fears. Sure he's probably after meeting some girl, we told him, and he's busy making the most of his last few hours in Stockholm with her. After all, given the choice between sharing a few hours with a pretty Swedish girl and spending all day drinking in a pub with a bunch of Irish lads in soccer and rugby jerseys, most of us would have picked the former. We sang the songs and drank the whiskey, but all the while Karl was checking his phone for a message that would never come.

As the days wore on and everyone began to fear the worst, Karl was inundated with offers of help and support. I didn't know John but as I spoke Swedish and knew plenty of people in the media, I offered to help in whatever way I could. When John's body was finally discovered some ten days later, I was convinced that two things had to happen. The first was that I was going to stop drinking.

I had always been a heavy enough drinker since my teens; perhaps not the last to leave the pub but never the first to turn down a jar if it was offered. Like most Irish lads I had found myself in plenty of scrapes in my time, but thankfully I'd never wound up in a situation that I couldn't get myself out of. But in truth, John's fate could have befallen any of us that were out that weekend. Given that I had two small children at home, enough was enough.

The second was that we would have to build a much stronger Irish community than we had before. Sure, we knew each other and met in the pubs and at Christmas time, but there was no real sense of belonging among the younger generation, even those who had lived here for five years or more. If we were to be able to speak with one voice and support each other in good times and in bad, it would require something stronger than the bonds forged on a Friday night in the pub and then forgotten by Saturday morning. To do so we would have to find some common ground, and like the vast majority of Irish villages, we would find that common ground on the playing field.

At the prize-giving ceremony following the Gothenburg tournament, I was rather disappointed that no trophy had been presented to us for winning the Scandinavian championship. I was sure that one existed from previous years and half-expected it would be produced and handed over by last year's winners, Malmö. But having received the trophy for the tournament victory from Billy, no more was forthcoming so we left it at that. Besides, with new clubs joining the tournament all the time, maybe it was time for a new one.

As no one else was going to give us one, we decided to go ahead and get our own trophy and medals which the Ambassador would present to us. The decision on what to call it was pretty unanimous, but given the sensitive nature of the subject, we had to be careful so as not to cause any offence.

I felt it was only fair to tell Karl in person that we wanted to name the trophy in John's memory, and that we also wanted him to make sure this was OK with John's family. We didn't want to just assume it would be. They might not like to be reminded of the tragic circumstances of his death. Maybe they wouldn't want John's name mentioned in the same breath as Stockholm ever again.

I finally buttonholed Karl as the Gaels gathered to support Tracey Sweeney at the opening of her art exhibition in a gallery in downtown Stockholm. A few of them may have been artists on the pitch, but none of them could match Tracey's talent off it, and by the end of its run every piece in the exhibition had been sold.

True to form, Karl and a couple of the boys were due to run a 10 or 20 kilometre road race later in the day, and he was dressed in his running kit when I brought him outside the gallery to ask if he thought this was a good idea. I could have sworn that the Sundbyberg Express welled up a little when I told him of our decision as a wave of sadness and pride washed over him. From the look on his face I knew for sure that this was the right thing to do. He told me later that the moment he felt tired in that race, he thought of John and the trophy, and he ran like he had never run before.

Ciarán was the last man to collect his medal, the wounded knee sustained back at the Malmö tournament not hindering him from accepting it from the ambassador. Then came the bittersweet moment we had all been waiting for, and which some of us had been dreading. I collected myself to speak for the last time that day.

'Ladies and gentlemen, there is a story behind the trophy that is about to be presented. I'm not going to say anything about it now, or why it received the name it did. There are others here who can tell you that story in a more dignified time and place.' I could feel the tears burning behind my eyes, and my voice was starting to shake, but this was one time I wasn't going to choke. 'In a break with tradition, I'm going to ask our captain Kevin Carroll to stand aside and allow our vice-captain Karl Lambert to accept the trophy from the ambassador.'

Karl stepped forward nervously, drying his palms as he approached the ambassador, as if he was afraid that the nervous sweat on his palms would make him drop it on his toes as soon as it was handed to him.

Ever the professional, Ambassador Hamill saw Karl's nerves and spoke to him softly. He shook his hand warmly for the second time that day before handing him the John Aherne trophy. 'Ladies and gentlemen, the champions of Scandinavia, the Stockholm Gaels,' I said, as Karl raised the trophy over his head in triumph.

An ear-splitting roar went up in the room as the camera flashes blinded the players, and in a split second it all became worth it. Every training session, every phone call, every email, every sleepless night, every injury, every single one of the millions of tiny details and problems we had faced during the season paled into insignificance. I looked at Karl and he looked back at me. No words were necessary, and together we crossed the room back to where our team mates stood waiting for the photographs to be taken.

The party looked like it was set to continue, but not for me. There were antibiotics and painkillers waiting at home, and my two daughters Ingrid and Freia had displayed great patience throughout the evening, but now it was time to go. I gathered up my belongings and said my goodbyes, thanking the ambassador and Ragnar once again for having us.

We walk back down to the waterside where the car is parked, and as the kids are getting in and putting on their seatbelts I stare into the cold, black water for a few seconds. 'Come on, dad, we're hungry.'

I get into the car and take one last look up at the windows of the chancery. The ambassador said he expected the reception to be finished by half past six, and he was probably right. The reception might be finished, but the party was only starting at the embassy. As I drove away I hoped he wasn't in any hurry home.